Praise for *Friend-Wise*

Friend-Wise is the kind of book we all need right now. With warmth, honesty, and biblical wisdom, Becky Harling offers both encouragement and practical tools for cultivating the friendships our souls long for. I've learned so much from Becky about being a great friend both through her words and through the way she lives her life. Whether you're longing for deeper community, healing from disappointment, or simply wanting to grow as a more intentional, loving friend, this book will be a helpful guide.

Crystal Paine, *New York Times* bestselling author, founder of MoneySavingMom.com and host of the *Crystal Paine Show*

Friend-Wise is a comforting, wise, and joy-filled guide for anyone longing to build meaningful, life-giving friendships. Becky Harling writes with a warm and gentle ease, pairing biblical wisdom with practical insight that actually works in real life. This book is a gift to every woman who has ever felt lonely, disconnected, or unsure of where to begin.

Jennifer Dukes Lee, author of *How to Love Your Morning* and *Growing Slow*

In an era of fake smiles and quick texts, Becky dares us to show up fully for friendship, without losing our minds or forgetting to laugh. *Friend-Wise* is packed with practical biblical wisdom and real-life stories to help you cultivate the iron-sharpening-iron relationships your heart actually needs. Becky lives out the principle she teaches—she's the real deal and a trusted voice on friendship.

Jenny Randle, ministry founder of the Holy Spirit Ministry Center and multi-published author, including *The Promised Presence*

Friend-Wise isn't a book you read once; it's a book you reference repeatedly. The short, topical chapters helped me identify my relational blind spots, then gave me actionable ways to pursue measurable growth in those areas. I'm getting copies for my friends so we can read it together!

Lisa Anderson, Director of Young Adults at Focus on the Family; author of *The Dating Manifesto*

With warmth, wisdom, and grace, Becky invites readers to cultivate the kind of friendships our hearts long for—authentic, life-giving, and rooted in godly love. Through personal stories, biblical truth, and practical guidance, she helps us deepen our connection with God and one another. Every woman longing for richer relationships will be refreshed and encouraged by this book.

Rachael Adams, author of *Everyday Prayers for Love* and host of *The Love Offering Podcast*

Like a strong cup of coffee in a favorite mug, Becky offers us a strong dose of courage for our friendships with the much-needed touch of gentleness. It's obvious this spills over from her time and rich friendship with Jesus, who offers us the truth we need with the grace we must have to be able to receive it. When it's so easy to focus on the other person in friendship, Becky leads us to focus on ourselves, surrendering our thoughts and cares to Christ through the authority of Scripture. These words God has given her were healing for me, bringing me clarity and wisdom while the Holy Spirit led me to the conviction and confessions awaiting me as I dared look within. The prayers help us as we move forward, becoming the godly friends we are called to be!

Candace Cofer, author, speaker, host of the *Good Day* podcast

In *Friend-Wise*, Becky Harling poignantly blends scriptural wisdom with heartfelt honesty, offering an evergreen guide for anyone longing for deeper, healthier friendships. Her words feel like warm coffee with a trusted friend—grace-filled, applicable, and real. Every chapter invites readers to pause, reflect, and pursue relationships that mirror the love and wisdom of Christ. This book isn't just about friendship; it's about becoming the kind of friend our hearts were made to be.

Amber Ginter Johnson, teacher-turned-author, speaker, mental health advocate, and host of the *Authentically Amber Podcast*

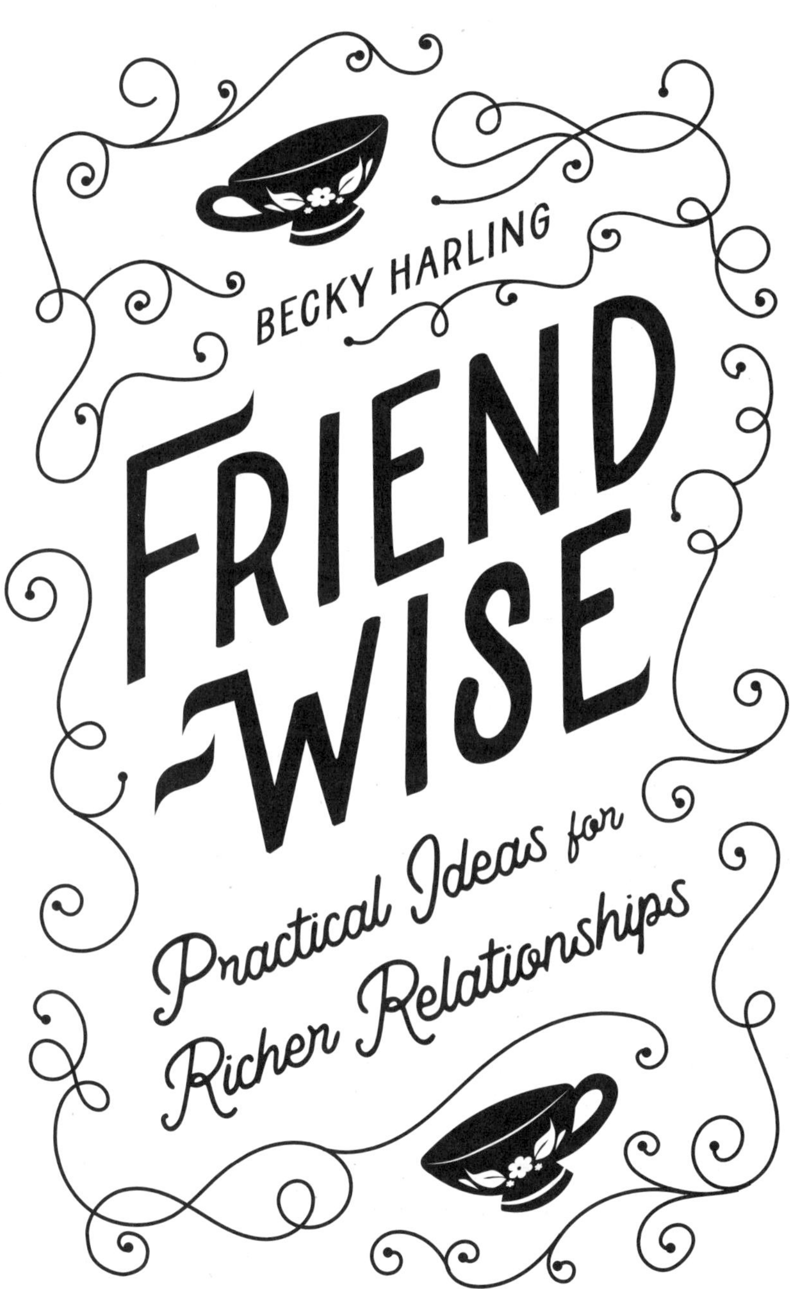

MOODY PUBLISHERS
CHICAGO

All emphasis in Scripture has been added.

Names and details of some stories have been changed to protect the privacy of individuals.

Published in association with The Blythe Daniel Agency.

Edited by Amanda Cleary Eastep
Interior design: Puckett Smartt
Cover design: Kaylee Lockenour Dunn
Author photo: Ashlee Kay Weaver

Library of Congress Cataloging-in-Publication Data

Names: Harling, Becky, 1957- author
Title: Friend-wise : practical ideas for deeper relationships / Becky Harling.
Description: Chicago : Moody Publishers, [2026] | Includes bibliographical references. | Summary: "Friendwise takes us to the fount of wisdom-the Proverbs-to guide us in cultivating stronger relationships. Becky teaches friendship skills, sharing wisdom on: Loyalty and guarding your heart. Contentment. Vulnerability. Forgiveness. Generosity. Encouragement. Criticism. Envy. Telling and speaking the truth. Apologizing. Trying to impress. Defensiveness. Dignity. And much more"-- Provided by publisher.
Identifiers: LCCN 2025032810 (print) | LCCN 2025032811 (ebook) | ISBN 9780802434715 paperback | ISBN 9780802470683 ebook
Subjects: LCSH: Bible. Proverbs--Criticism, interpretation, etc. | Friendship--Biblical teaching | Interpersonal relations--Biblical teaching | BISAC: RELIGION / Christian Living / Devotional | RELIGION / Christian Living / Spiritual Growth
Classification: LCC BS1465.6.F73 H37 2026 (print) | LCC BS1465.6.F73 (ebook)
LC record available at https://lccn.loc.gov/2025032810
LC ebook record available at https://lccn.loc.gov/2025032811

Originally delivered by fleets of horse-drawn wagons, the affordable paperbacks from D. L. Moody's publishing house resourced the church and served everyday people. Now, after more than 125 years of publishing and ministry, Moody Publishers' mission remains the same—even if our delivery systems have changed a bit. For more information on other books (and resources) created from a biblical perspective, go to www.moodypublishers.com or write to:

Moody Publishers
820 N. LaSalle Boulevard
Chicago, IL 60610

1 3 5 7 9 10 8 6 4 2

Printed in the United States of America

This book is lovingly dedicated to my wise friend, Gayle Call.
Love you dearly and am so grateful for our friendship!

CONTENTS

How Are You Doing, Friend-Wise?

Recently, after listening to someone who poured out her heart about a lot of chaos in her life, I asked the simple question, "How are you doing friend-wise?" There was a long pause. She responded, "I mean, I have friends, but at times I feel lonely and disconnected. I feel like everyone is so busy. I long for richer relationships, but sometimes, I'm not sure how to move forward."

At different seasons in our lives, we've all felt like that.

Maybe it's a season where you are homebound with young children. Or maybe you've just moved to a different geographic area and you're having trouble finding friends and connecting. Perhaps you've recently walked a journey of grief, and you lack the energy to reach out and initiate. Whatever the reason, let me ask *you*, how are you doing friend-wise? Are your friendships filled with delight? Do they bring you joy or are they draining? Do you feel connected and like you are enjoying a good, supportive community? These are good questions to consider.

According to research, it has been determined that spending time with friends you like increases your happiness as much as if you had a $133,000 raise per year![1] If that's true, we'd better figure out how to do it, because who doesn't need a little happiness?

We have myriad relationships: acquaintances, parents (some of us have aging parents); we may have a spouse and children; extended family, and work relationships. Among all the people we feel responsible for, how do we nurture our friendships so that we enjoy the richness of those deep connections?

As followers of Jesus, we want to be people filled with godly wisdom and discernment in all our relationships. We want to love others well and enjoy great friendships, like Jesus. Yet at times, we wonder what that looks like. Jesus Himself said, "I have called you friends" (John 15:15). He invites us to friendship with Him and then invites us to enter into rich friendships with others.

We need girlfriends to surround us and sustain us in the wonkiness of life. I believe we need friends who are a bit older than us to bring wise counsel. We need friends in our particular season who share common interests that we can enjoy. We need diverse friends who bring new perspectives to our lives, and we need younger friends who we are seeking to encourage. On top of that, if we're married, we need to cultivate friendship with our spouse. We might know that, but maybe we lack the wisdom to move forward.

James, the brother of Jesus, wrote, "If any of you lacks wisdom, you should ask God, who gives generously to all without finding fault, and it will be given to you" (James 1:5). What a promise! If we need wisdom, we can ask, and God will answer. But what is wisdom anyway? And how does it apply to friendships? James went on to describe godly wisdom: "The wisdom that comes from heaven is first of all pure; then peace-loving, considerate, submissive, full of mercy and good fruit, impartial and sincere. Peacemakers who sow in peace reap a harvest of righteousness" (James 3:17–18).

The Hebrew word for wisdom is *hokmach*, and interestingly enough, means "skill."[2] We need appropriate social skills to navigate our many relationships. Recently, my little granddaughter came home from a play date that she felt shy about attending. At first, she was not at all sure she wanted to go. But when she came home, she said to her mom proudly, "I practiced my social skills." I love that! Out of the mouth of babes, right? During different seasons of life, it's good to ask, "Am I practicing my social skills? How am I doing friend-wise?"

In this short book, we'll focus on practical ideas to help you deepen and enhance your friendships. In our current epidemic of loneliness, who doesn't want their relationships to go deeper? So come on and take this journey with me. There are thirty skills in all. And let me just say, there's no timeline for this book. Read it fast or read it slow—whatever works with your lifestyle. It might be that you look up which skill you need for a particular season. That's fine.

Each short chapter will include:

- a verse from Proverbs
- brief illustrations/anecdotes
- a relational truth for the day
- a reflective question
- a prayer

Throughout the book, you will find quotes describing good friends. These are all from friends of mine but will give you some food for thought.

Know that I am praying for you! My prayer is that God will use this little book to help your friendships flourish and grow, and that as a result, you will experience the joy of a deeply connected life.

CHAPTER 1

Be Intentional

For the waywardness of the simple will kill them,
and the complacency of fools will destroy them.
PROVERBS 1:32

I remember my cancer journey quite well. As I rested on the couch day after day trying to recuperate from surgeries, I remember considering the question, "What's most important in my life?" As I wrestled with that question, I came to three conclusions: My relationship with God was most important, and I would not grow complacent in that relationship. I would invest by spending time in prayer, worship, and Bible meditation. No longer would I allow *doing* for God to trump *being* with God. I wanted the deepest relationship I could possibly have with Him, and that meant I had to be intentional.

Secondly, I determined my family was next in importance. I committed to spending more time listening to and encouraging each member. And finally, I determined my friendships were important. No longer would I run at such a fast pace that I wouldn't have time for a deep conversation with friends. I needed to create space in my life to invest in friendships. Looking back, cancer was very clarifying.

I began to make changes immediately, beginning with prioritizing unhurried time with friends. Prior to cancer, my beliefs about ministry life got in the way of friendships. When I was training to go into ministry, I was often told not to get too close to people in our church. Honestly, that was messed up! If you don't get close to people where you are ministering, you lead a very lonely life. After I was cancer free, I began being much more intentional in enjoying my friends. My husband stepped into a new church, and rather than following old advice on maintaining distance in ministry, I dove into deeper friendships with those in the church. They are still my friends today.

I also learned to slow down. On a practical level I started listening more intently when I was on the phone with friends. Rather than feeling like I needed to hurry to get other stuff done. I simply reminded myself that I had plenty of time to listen.

One time, I met up with a dear friend in New York City. From JFK International Airport, we took a train into the city to see a Broadway show. I had never spent money to simply be with a friend before. That time ended up being so great for my soul! I became intentional about choosing vulnerability and being more authentic in my friendships.

Rather than just waiting for friends to pop into my life, I went after them. I took the initiative to invite others out for coffee and to go to lunch. Looking back, these were some of the most positive choices I ever made. I realized how vital life-giving friendships are.

The same holds true for you. Your friendships are vital. If you grow busy and ignore your friends for too long, your connection will drift and eventually die.

Scripture reminds us that "the complacency of fools will destroy them" (Prov. 1:32). That seems a bit strong, don't you think? I mean, life gets busy, and we get hurried. At times, we're emotionally exhausted from the sheer amount of chaos our lives involve. You might be wondering, "What's wrong with a little complacency?"

What exactly is complacency? Complacency is an attitude of apathy. It shows up in passivity and ultimately dishonors those we claim to love. When we are complacent, we are listless and apathetic because we simply don't care. We no longer want to put effort into our friendship with God or others. Ultimately, complacency is self-indulgent and kills our friendships.

The prophet Zephaniah gave us insight into how God feels about complacency. Speaking the Lord's words, he wrote, "At that time I will search Jerusalem with lamps and punish those who are complacent" (Zeph. 1:12).

In Matthew 25:14–30, Jesus tells the story of servants who have been given bags of gold: One servant was given five, one was given two, and one was given one bag of gold. The master who handed out the money went on a trip, trusting his servants to invest his money wisely. When he returned, the servant who had been given five bags had invested and gained five more. The one who had been given two invested and he also doubled what he had been entrusted with. However, the one to whom one had been given simply buried the bag so he wouldn't have to worry. When the master came back, he affirmed the two who had been intentional with their bags of gold, but he was furious with the one who had buried his. In fact, he called him wicked! This story teaches us to be intentional with the gifts we have been given and industrious until the return of Jesus, our trustworthy Master. We might also look to this story as an analogy for complacency with what has been entrusted to us. Beyond talents or financial resources, one of the gifts God entrusts us with is our friendships. I believe He wants us to invest in these relationships and treasure them.

How Does Complacency Show Up in Our Friendships?

It can show up as being too busy to nurture your friendships. It can show up as a lack of empathy when your friend is struggling. It can show up as building walls around our heart so that we never have to risk getting hurt again. Or it can even show up as taking friends for granted.

God wants us to treasure our friendships with the wisdom of intentionality. Let's ask Him to show us where we've grown complacent in our friendships.

Friendship Wisdom

Be intentional and view your friends as treasures. Take one intentional step. Write a note to a friend saying how much you appreciate their friendship. Or treat a friend to coffee or lunch. During your time together, tell them about the qualities in their life that you appreciate.

Pause and Reflect

Has complacency crept into your friendships? How can you be more intentional? What needs to change from your perspective?

Prayer

Lord God, I praise You that You invite me to be intentional in my friendships with others. Thank You that You are always intentional to pursue me and You call me Your friend. Help me to treasure my friendships and never take them for granted. I pray that You would uproot complacency in my life in all my relationships. Help me to steward the friendships You give me well. Be glorified through me, I pray.

"A good friend is someone who loves you in the practical, nitty gritty, messy kind of way: The friend who brings chicken soup when your family's hit with the flu. The friend who answers your SOS text and prays you through a crisis. The friend who lets you see her own joys and struggles so you both know you're not alone."

Asheritah Ciuciu

Author, Speaker, and Bible Teacher

CHAPTER 2

Tune In

Turning your ear to wisdom
and applying your heart to understanding.
PROVERBS 2:2

Our youngest daughter, Keri, landed the role of Cinderella in the youth theater production. She was wildly excited and did an amazing job. However, one night she had a severe asthma attack before the show. If you have a child with asthma, you know this can be scary! She had already used her inhaler, but her breathing was not slowing down, and she was beginning to panic, which makes asthma worse. Our older daughter, Stefanie, calmly stepped in and put her hand on Keri's chest; then she took Keri's hand and put it on her own chest. "Keri, let's breathe together," Stefanie said. They slowly took deep breaths and exhaled, simultaneously. Gradually, by breathing in rhythm with Stefanie, Keri's asthma was quieted. That is a beautiful picture of attunement.

Attunement is a popular concept within the realm of relationships. It means that we are tuned in to another's emotions, feelings, and needs. This leads to stronger connection between two people. Attunement weans us off of words alone. We stop talking as much and do more listening and observing. This allows us to offer the gift of our full presence to another.

However, if we don't calm and quiet our own souls, we can't be attuned to others. That's where the rub comes for most of us. We have so much clamoring in our minds that it becomes challenging to quiet our thoughts and fully focus on another to offer our full presence. Yet, to be a good friend, we must learn how to do this.

King Solomon instructed that we are to turn our hearts toward wisdom and apply our hearts to understanding. The place where this begins is with God. We must attune to Him first in order to find wisdom and be able to offer our full presence to others.

When we attune to God, we become still. We know that He is God and we become more aware of His presence. We learn to slow our souls and breathe in rhythm with His heartbeat. If we want wisdom in our relationships, we must attune to God first and then ask for the grace to attune to others.

Often, we don't understand what our friends are feeling because we haven't gotten quiet enough to attune to.

How Do We Attune to Others?

Practice times of silence. We live in a world full of distractions. We've grown accustomed to a constant undercurrent of noise. For our brains to recalibrate and be able to tune in effectively to God and others, we need spaces of quiet. In our silence, we can seek to get our hearts and breath in sync with God. Before we can effectively bring understanding to our friendships, we need to be in harmony with God. And the thing is, we can't be present to God without getting quiet. This is why the psalmist wrote, "Be still, and know that I am God" (Ps. 46:10).

Think about Elijah in the Old Testament trying to hear God's voice. God's voice was not in the powerful wind, it was not in the earthquake, and it was not in the fire. God's wisdom came to Elijah in a quiet whisper.

(See 1 Kings 19:11–13.) How often might we miss God's wisdom because we are simply never quiet or still?

Learn to be attentive to another's body language. To be a good friend and offer understanding, you must learn to be attuned to another person's body language. This takes a bit of practice, but it is achievable. If you practice focusing on your friend's expressions and movements, you can pick up clues as to what they are feeling and what they need in the moment. If you're with your friend and their body appears tense, chances are they're feeling stressed. If they're talking wildly fast, they might feel anxious. Learn the signals that you can attune effectively.

Bring your full presence. We are such a distracted culture that this takes continual work for all of us. I'm working on this as well. The key distraction in my life is my phone. A while back I was at lunch with a friend, enjoying rich conversation, and my phone rang three times. My friend finally invited me to pick it up, which I did only to realize my hubby wanted to know what was for dinner. Since that time, I've learned to turn my phone on silent when I'm out with friends so that I am not distracted. When I'm with friends, I want to be fully present. I want to be able to not only hear what they're saying, I want to observe and feel what they're feeling. The only way we can attune to friends is if we are fully present with them. And for many of us that means turning off our phones.

Friendship Wisdom

Learn to practice attunement to both God and your friends.

Pause and Reflect

How often do you get quiet before God and embrace silence?

Prayer

Lord God, my world is such a noisy place. Constant notifications on my phone, the continual noise of the TV, persistent differing opinions, and the perpetual clutter of thoughts all distract me from embracing quiet and tuning my heart to hear Your voice. Holy Spirit, quiet my heart. Help me today to tune my ear to hear Your voice and then fill me with the ability to attune to my friends' hearts. Show me what it looks like to offer others my full presence today. Help me to be aware of their body language and what they might need in a given moment.

"A good friend is someone who holds space in their life for me by listening to understand, speaking to encourage, and being present emotionally and physically."

SAUNDRA DALTON SMITH

Author, Speaker, and Coach

CHAPTER 3

Be Faithful

Let love and faithfulness never leave you;
bind them around your neck,
write them on the tablet of your heart.
PROVERBS 3:3

I was seated on a plane headed to a speaking event, and I happened to be sitting next to an elderly couple. The wife began talking to me immediately. She was delightful! We shared a love for coffee, and she told me in great detail how she most enjoyed the first cup of the day as well as a cup after supper. The perfect way to begin and end her day. She was my kind of friend. I couldn't agree more! I love that first early morning sip as I head to my knees at the beginning of each day. Coffee is the great connector.

My new friend then went on to tell me that she and her husband had been married for seventy-two years. It turns out they were both in their nineties; they had married at the age of eighteen. Many had told them they were too young and that it would never last. She leaned in close to me and whispered, "I knew it was going to last because I determined no matter what happened, I wasn't leaving. I was going to cultivate loyalty and faithfulness." We finished our conversation talking about kids, grandkids, and her great-grandkids. What a beautiful conversation we had as we flew. I left the plane feeling inspired by my new friend's loyalty.

Loyalty in relationships is often a forgotten quality in our culture. If a marriage is struggling, partners opt out. If a friendship has a rift, friends put distance between each other rather than doing the hard work of repairing. The problem is that without faithfulness, our relationships will never grow deep enough for us to feel fully connected.

Solomon counsels us to prioritize love and faithfulness in our relationships. (See Proverbs 3:3.) He goes so far as to say that we engrave them on our hearts. What does this look like in our lives?

It will take several practices to cultivate faithfulness in our relationships.

The first practice is to learn to work through conflict. I can hear you, and I resonate. I hate conflict. However, in every friendship, there will be a measure of friction or conflict. For some of us, conflict is challenging and even scary. But if we change our mindset and view conflict as a path to deeper friendship, we find the courage to work things out. When you have a different opinion, focus your listening on understanding the other person's perspective. Offering understanding goes a long way in resolving differences.

The second practice is to prioritize steadfastness. Faithfulness and steadfastness are similar. They remain even when the relationship is strained. Love is not just a feeling; it's also a choice to value the other person. In your friendships, learn to continually go back to the Holy Spirit and ask Him to love through you. In that way, you become a conduit of love to your friends, neighbors, and coworkers. Every person is made in the image of God. When friends walk through rough waters, stay. Often, we don't mean to ditch out; we just become too busy to stay engaged. Ask the Lord to strengthen you to be encouraging.

The third practice is forgiveness. Every friendship will include hurt at some point. We get hurt and then we make meaning in our heads. I remember when a friend of mine told me some things that really hurt my feelings. I didn't process it with her. I kept it inside and I started to spin stories in my head. That's when, thankfully, I turned to prayer and asked the Holy Spirit to give me wisdom. He showed me that I needed to simply let it go and offer my friend grace. She hadn't meant to hurt me and likely still doesn't even know she hurt me. I simply had to let it go and forgive, remembering how precious the friendship was to me.

Friendship Wisdom

Prioritize faithfulness in your friendships.* Be faithful and consistent in reaching out to your friends. Forgive whenever the opportunity arises.

Pause and Reflect

How many friends do you have with whom you've been in a relationship for years, even decades? Those friendships are treasures.

Prayer

Lord Jesus, I praise You for Your love and faithfulness. Thank You for the friendships You've brought into my life. Help me to echo Your love and faithfulness to them. Fill me with Your Holy Spirit today and strengthen my loyalty muscles. Help me to be a faithful friend to many. May Your love fill me today and flow out of my life so that all who come in contact with me will feel Your presence.

* Please note: The exception to this is if you are in an abusive relationship. Then you need to seek godly counsel for how to escape. God does not want you to be abused.

"A good friend takes time to truly know you and your heart and continues to faithfully love you."

Keri Spring

CEO of Greg Spring Foundation

CHAPTER 4

Guard Your Self-Talk

Above all else, guard your heart,
for everything you do flows from it.
PROVERBS 4:23

I used to think the phrase "guard your heart" was about constructing walls around your heart to keep immoral people and bad influences out. I was raised in a culture where that was taught. After further study, I realized that this verse refers to our thought life, the narratives we tell ourselves. That's a whole other issue, right?

"In the Old Testament, the word 'heart' is used more than eight hundred times, but more than two hundred times it deals with one's thought life, emotions, the wellsprings of life, those things that motivate and mold us."[1] In this way, guarding our hearts involves much more than simply not hanging around with immoral people. The truth is, Jesus hung around with immoral people all the time. It's our thought life He's concerned about.

Our thoughts can distract us from focusing completely on Christ. Let me give you an example. I woke up early to spend time with Jesus. But as I was trying to spend time in prayer, my anxious thoughts went rogue. I thought about all the tasks I had to accomplish that day. I thought about several of my grandkids who had recently experienced sickness. I thought through my upcoming schedule and wondered if I could keep up. I worried over a few relationships that felt off to me. Ever have a morning like that?

Finally, mercifully, it dawned on me that I needed to guard my heart against a tsunami of fear and anxiety. I needed to capture every thought and wrangle it to submit so that, as Solomon writes, I could let my eyes "look straight ahead" into the wonderful face of Jesus. (See Proverbs 4:25.)

Our thoughts can also get us into trouble in our friendships. When we create meaning in our minds about someone else's actions, we are on shaky ground. We can never completely know another person's motives, yet we imagine scenarios all the time. A friend cancels on lunch, and we think, "She doesn't value the friendship as much as I do." In truth, it might not have anything to do with you.

Friend, making up stories in our minds about someone else's motives is very dangerous. We must, in the words of the apostle Paul, learn to "take every thought captive" (2 Cor. 10:5). We must learn to put a fence around our thoughts and learn the power of containing them.

How Do We Guard Our Hearts and Take Every Thought Captive in Our Relationships?

Capture rogue thoughts. When your mind goes to all the "what ifs" you need to pull rank. You have authority over your thought life. We are created in the image of God and, as such, are the only created creatures with the ability to direct our thoughts. Rather than spiraling down into a pit of anxiety and fear, capture your thoughts and redirect them to what's true about God. (See Philippians.) As you fix your focus on Him, calm and clear thinking will replace confusion and chaos.

Learn to clarify meaning. Rather than assuming you know what a friend is thinking, ask that person to clarify. Be vulnerable enough to ask, "What I think you mean is________. Is that correct?" Author Pete Scazzero puts it this way, "If we are to respect and love others as Jesus did, it is essential to refrain from assuming we know what others are thinking."[2] This is an easy bad habit to get into. Unfortunately, it will create havoc in your friendships.

Assume the best about people. In our polarized culture, we often assume the worst about people. Instead, guard your heart against negative and critical thoughts toward others and assume the best. Rather than viewing people as annoyances or as enemies of our Christianity, we need to view them as humans created in the image of God, whom God Himself dearly loves! Every person is worth treating with dignity. Take every thought captive. Choose to love others well and to view them through God's eyes rather than your own.

Friendship Wisdom

Take control of your thought life and clarify meaning with your friends rather than assuming their motives.

Pause and Reflect

When have you recently assumed someone's motives, only to discover their motives were completely different? How did you clarify your own thoughts?

Prayer

Holy Spirit, cleanse my heart. I pray that You would bring my mind into alignment with the mind of Christ. May I think His thoughts about others. Help me to love others well, to viewing them as wonderful humans created in the image of God Himself. May I grant each person I meet today dignity and value.

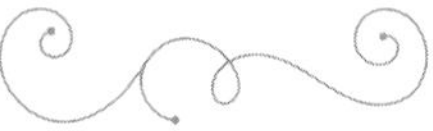

"A good friend loves through honest conversation."

PAT LAYTON

Author, Speaker, Coach

CHAPTER 5

Cultivate Contentment

Drink water from your own cistern,
running water from your own well.
PROVERBS 5:15

I've previously told the story of a conversation I had with my granddaughter, who at the time was eleven. When I asked her what God was teaching her, Selah paused and then said, "Contentment!"[1] Wow! I was floored. She went on to say that she was content with who God had made her, and she was content with the gifts and abilities God had given her. To learn contentment at such a young age is incredible and will bode well for Selah as she grows older. Honestly, she's ahead of most adults I know.

One of the lies of our culture is the myth of "greener grass," which tells us that what someone has is better than what you have, and you are entitled to happiness. As a result, many are simply never content. They want a different house or a different spouse. They want more money and more possessions. They want a better body and stronger gifts, and they feel they are entitled to it all. However, their souls are never settled or at peace. It is hard to be friends with someone who is never content. God calls us to cultivate contentment in all areas of our lives.

Contentment means trusting that God's provision is enough.

It sounds easy. However, for most, it is a lifelong journey. We must learn contentment through the constant submission to the will of God. We embrace God's will for our lives in all areas, including our relationships. Now, don't get me wrong, this doesn't mean you don't work to learn new people skills, it means that you bow your expectations of others to the Lord, and make peace with the fact that you cannot change others.

It's not wrong to want certain things in our relationships. We all have desires (Ps. 37:4). Contentment doesn't mean we deny that those desires are present. Nor does it mean we "fake it till we make it." Contentment invites us to be honest about what we need and want, but to trust God with our longings.

I remember a season in my life when I felt jealous of my friends' houses. We lived in a fairly small house with four kids and a dog. The house was a great provision; it's just that it didn't feel like enough. As I looked at my friends who all had houses that were large and beautiful, I felt my longings for a bigger house grow. I'm not saying that was wrong, it's just that it started impacting my friendships. I felt like I wanted to distance myself from those who had better homes. I had to sit with the Lord and ask Him to change my heart because many people are going to have bigger homes than me. I needed to nurture contentment.

Maybe you're not wrestling with jealousy over your friend's house, but you sure wish your kids were as well-behaved as hers. Or you wish your husband were as helpful around the house or as romantic as your friend's husband. Be careful when those thoughts come because they are dangerous! Stop comparing and instead start praising God for what you do have in your family.

I have known friends who, when their marriage felt lacking, turned to greener pastures. Those stories never end well. They cause immeasurable damage to both the partner who cheats and the partner who is betrayed. This is why Solomon wrote, "Drink water from your own cistern, running water from your own well" (Prov. 5:15). Blessings come to those who find contentment in what the Lord has provided.

Beyond marriage, our friendships will benefit from our contentment. A soul at rest makes a wonderful friend. When we are content with what God has given and allowed in our lives, we don't place extraordinary expectations on others. We don't continually compare and become offended easily. We are less likely to complain and be negative. Honestly, it is very challenging to be friends with someone who is always discontent with their life. Those who are satisfied are a joy to be around. Others feel lifted and encouraged when they're with them. They feel inspired to cultivate contentment in their own lives.

Paul wrote to his mentee Timothy: "Godliness with contentment is great gain" (1 Tim. 6:6). Though contentment is not easily gained, it is worth the struggle to get there. Paul also wrote that he had learned the secret to being content (Phil. 4:11). Part of the secret is to stop complaining and grumbling (Phil. 2:14). Complaining is not the same as grieving. Grieving loss is legitimate and godly. There are things in life worth weeping over. Grumbling is different. Listen to yourself intentionally for a day and keep track of what you complain about: the weather, the price of food, the government, the annoying person at work. There are endless opportunities to gripe and complain. But it is annoying to others. So, stop. Contentment comes slowly, but when you grumble and gripe, you slow down the process even more.

When you're with your friends, let go of complaining. Seek to be a person that others find life-giving. Ask the Holy Spirit to develop contentment in you. Practice gratitude. Praise and thank God that He is enough in every situation. Even in the difficulties of life, learn to enjoy His presence above all else. The richer your relationship with Jesus, the less you will struggle with discontent. When you are tempted to complain or grumble, choose praise instead.

Friendship Wisdom

Rather than complaining, cultivate gratitude to increase your contentment.

Pause and Reflect

What do you most often complain about? How would your friendships be different if you were content?

Prayer

> *Lord Jesus, when I am tempted to gripe or complain, fill me with contentment instead. I realize it is so easy to fall into destructive patterns of complaining about everything. As I learn to cultivate contentment in my life, I realize I will be able to offer a more peaceful presence to my friends. Pour through me, I pray, so that I might bless my friends by being life-giving rather than dragging them down with negativity. Fill my sight with glimpses of Your goodness so that I might focus on that rather than on what I lack.*

CHAPTER 6

Apologize Authentically

[If] you have been trapped by what you said, ensnared by the words of your mouth. . . . Go—to the point of exhaustion.

Proverbs 6:2–3

I was tired and a bit cranky after a long and grueling ministry trip. On the trip, I saw attitudes that frustrated me. As a result, I lashed out at my friend. I became accusatory and judgmental. Later, after a lot of rest, I realized how awful my words had been. I had to go back and apologize and ask for forgiveness.

Another time, a friend was processing some different job opportunities. Without letting her finish, I dove in and gave unsolicited advice. I know better. I know that people are looking for a listening ear, not for a friend to solve all their problems. Nonetheless, my mouth got the better of me. I had to go back and humbly apologize for offering advice that wasn't requested. Thankfully, my friend is good at offering grace.

If you want strong friendships, you need to honestly take a look at when you've blown it and humbly offer a sincere apology.

Too often, people apologize with excuses for their behavior. We may have heard these from a friend or even said these things ourselves: "Sorry, but I was just tired/hungry." Or, "Sorry you got your feelings hurt." Perhaps the worst apology I've heard is, "I'm sorry *if* I offended you." Think about it. That's not a genuine apology. Those apologies are not authentic. Instead, they are flippant and defensive. Fake apologies don't do the hard work of repairing the relationship. They don't rebuild a bridge to your friend's heart; they widen the distance between two people. A true apology always moves the relationship toward reconciliation.

Jesus said, "Blessed are the peacemakers" (Matt. 5:9). A peacemaker initiates reconciliation, but reconciliation never happens without heartfelt apologies. In light of that, we'd best figure out what it means to offer a genuine apology.

What Constitutes a Humble and Genuine Apology?

A genuine apology accepts responsibility for wrongdoing. In our human nature, we are so reticent to admit wrongdoing. A true apology not only admits fault but also takes responsibility for the hurt our error caused to another. Blame-shifting is a common pattern in our culture. However, we are called to be different. Even in the realm of minor mistakes, we still want to take responsibility for our own actions. Our relationships will grow deeper if we do.

A genuine apology shows sincere remorse. It's not enough to simply say a flippant, "I'm sorry"; it must come from a humble heart. Humility is one of the character traits that most reflects the heart of Christ. Paul reminds us that it is godly sorrow that brings repentance (2 Cor. 7:10). Our friendships are gifts from God. When we hurt someone or wrong them, we must choose to ask God for godly sorrow and apologize with sincere remorse.

A genuine apology shows a commitment to change. We may admit that we blew it, but do we feel remorseful enough to change our behavior? Scripture instructs, "Whoever conceals their sins does not prosper, but the one who confesses and renounces them finds mercy" (Prov. 28:13). I don't believe this verse is simply talking about our relationship to God. It's also giving us wise counsel for how to love others more effectively. If you want your friendships to thrive, you need to apologize and commit to change.

A genuine apology demonstrates the transformative power of the gospel in your life. Friend, when you came to Christ, you died to your old way of life, including arrogance. Pride is one of the sins that God hates the most. (See Prov. 6:16–17.) Humility is the way of Jesus. Admitting your faults and being willing to apologize are tangible ways to grow in humility and a sign that you are being transformed by Christ. If it's been a long time since you've apologized, you might consider: Is the gospel transforming your life?

The relational skill of apologizing and making amends is a challenging one. I get it—it's hard. It's not pleasant to admit we were wrong, say we're sorry, and change. However, if we are going to enjoy the deeply connected relationships that God intended, we must grow, be able to apologize, and make amends to repair broken relationships.

Friendship Wisdom

Practice the skill of genuinely apologizing when you hurt a friend's feelings. Be sure your apology communicates clearly that you are taking responsibility.

Pause and Reflect

As you think back on the last few months, when was the last time you truly experienced sorrow over hurting someone else, either with your words or your actions? Did you apologize? What does it look like to repair the relationship?

Prayer

Lord Jesus, I praise and thank You that You went to the cross so I could be reconciled with. Honestly, I feel within myself some defensiveness. It's often hard for me to admit my faults, apologize humbly, and make amends. Holy Spirit, change me. Create in me a clean heart and grant me a willing spirit to admit when I am wrong.

CHAPTER 7

Set Wise Boundaries

Keep my commands and you will live;
guard my teachings as the apple of your eye.
PROVERBS 7:2

The boundary lines have fallen for me in pleasant places.
PSALM 16:6

Feeling sick to my stomach, I scanned the congregation, mapping out my escape. Every head was bowed and every eye closed, so I snuck out of my pew to head for the bathrooms, which were behind the platform. I made it as far as the communion table, and that's when—and where—I "tossed my breakfast." I'm sure eyes popped wide, and mouths dropped open as every person in that congregation watched, horrified. The only eyes still closed were those of my fiancé, who kept right on praying.

Earlier that morning, Steve, then my fiancé, had pressured me into going to church with him. I had woken up with flu symptoms, but Steve felt desperate to have me come with him to candidate at the little country church. Against my better judgment, but longing to keep my fiancé happy, I agreed to go. What unfolded was a disaster of epic proportions that left me wildly embarrassed. Some women came forward and helped me clean up. Shockingly, the church voted Steve in 100 percent. To this day, we feel that it was a pity vote! When he first asked me to go with him, I should have lovingly told Steve no.

Soon after, we got married. I brought my people-pleasing nature right into our ministry life and my friendships. As a result, my wrestling with boundaries continued. When to say no and how to say no often left me confused and stressed out. Sometimes I said yes but then felt resentful. If we want healthy and happy friendships, we have to learn to embrace our limits and set boundaries.

The apostle Paul wrote to the Corinthian church, "Neither do we go beyond our limits by boasting of work done by others" (2 Cor. 10:16). Notice that phrase "beyond our limits." In this passage, Paul was speaking of the boundaries he put in place to not boast. If you want to be friend-wise, putting a boundary around boasting is a great idea! However, there are other areas we are not to go beyond our limits besides merely bragging. A good question to consider is where else in the realm of friendship do we tend to go beyond our limits? That will help you identify where you are most tempted to break your own boundaries.

What Are Boundaries and Why Are They Important in Friendships?

Boundaries are healthy limits. They make good neighbors, and they assure that your relationships stay emotionally and spiritually healthy. They define where you start and where another person ends. They are about taking responsibility for your own life.

Jesus modeled a life of boundaries. He only said yes to what the Father had asked Him. In Mark 1:24, a demon spoke out, identifying Jesus as the Holy One of God, but Jesus rebuked it and told it to be quiet!

Why? Because Jesus knew it wasn't the right time to reveal completely who He was. Later in the chapter (vv. 35–39), the disciples put pressure on Jesus because He was spending time with the Father, and everyone was looking for Him. I'm intrigued by how Jesus handled the pressure. He remained calm and simply said, "Let us go somewhere else." Jesus understood that if He was going to fulfill the mission God had for Him, He would have to keep boundaries in place.

Boundaries were God's idea, and they help us accept our limitations. They empower us to say no to what might even be good, to say yes to something better. When we continually cross our own boundary line, we may end up resenting the friends we said yes to. Ultimately, setting and keeping boundaries is essential for strong relationships.

If you wrestle with saying no to friends, here are a couple of suggestions.

Practice the "uncomplicated no." Our temptation when we *do* say no is to overexplain. Have you ever found yourself overexplaining to someone why you can't take on a new commitment, or why you can't attend an event, or why you didn't finish a project on time? Part of the simple no is simply not feeling the pressure to answer text messages immediately. It's okay to not answer right away. It's also fine to not pick up the phone if it's not a convenient time. These are simple ways to uncomplicate your life.

Friends, if we're going to exercise the skill of setting healthy boundaries, we have to simplify our no's. Simple answers include: "No, I'm unable to commit to that right now." Or, "No, I don't have the capacity for that in this season." Or simply waiting to answer text messages when it's convenient. Rather than delving into a long explanation, *simply say no*.

Quit being obsessed with what others think of you. Most people are not even thinking about you. They've got too much on their mind to be preoccupied with you. If this is something you worry about, ask the Holy Spirit to free you from it. You have enough to manage in your own mind. You don't need to worry about what's happening in other people's minds. Instead, fix your focus on Christ and occupy your thoughts with what He is calling you to do, even if you disappoint your friends.

Establishing boundaries can be a challenge; however, if we're going to enjoy emotionally healthy friendships, we have to put the work into creating and keeping healthy boundaries. The great news is that we have the Holy Spirit living within us, and He is more than willing to help us get this straight. As we find ourselves challenged in this area, we can cry out to Him and He will give us the wisdom to put boundaries in place—even in our closest friendships.

Friendship Wisdom

Next time you are feeling pressured to do something that you would rather not do, try saying "the uncomplicated no" without an explanation.

Pause and Reflect

In which relationships do you feel overwhelmed? Where are you exceeding your limits? How might setting better boundaries help you?

Prayer

Lord Jesus, I praise You that You set such a great example for me in the area of boundaries. While You were here on earth, You needed to sleep and eat and practice restraint. You didn't heal everybody, and at times You said no. Oh Lord, I love to keep others happy, but I realize it can exhaust me. Grant me the wisdom and the discipline to say no and to set boundaries in my life. May I live for Your applause alone!

CHAPTER 8

Discover the Deepest Source of Attachment

> *I was filled with delight day after day,*
> *rejoicing always in his presence.*
> PROVERBS 8:30

Becky, you should have deep attachment issues." My counselor's words reverberated in my head long after I left her office. She was right; my mother suffered from dark depression after I was born. When I was only a few weeks old, she left for a month on a ministry trip with my dad. My father, though in ministry, was abusive, so I could never quite trust him.

Therapists and counselors alike tell us that to form healthy attachments with others, we must bond with a trustworthy caregiver in infancy. However, what happens if you don't? Are you unable to attach for the rest of your life? I don't believe so. I believe that God offers us the most secure and healthy attachment. Out of that secure bonded attachment we are able to love and bond with friends. We love our friends out of the overflow of a secure heart. This is why it is essential to learn to enjoy and feel secure in God's presence.

For many, enjoying God's presence feels ethereal. Yet, it is the key to lasting joy and security. It doesn't have to be some weird ethereal experience. As I have grown in learning to enjoy God's presence, I have found some tools that help. Gary Thomas wrote a book called *Sacred Pathways*, which helps readers understand that each of us is wired differently as far as experiencing the presence of God. We can strengthen our friendships by learning to enjoy God's presence together.

For example, my friend Judy and I both love the outdoors. We have met together for times of prayer in the Garden of the Gods park. Another friend loves worship music like I do. She and I often get on our knees together to worship.

I experience the love and security of God's presence when I am on my knees early in the morning listening to worship music and allowing it to prompt my praise. As I spend time worshiping and praising God, I feel His presence come close, and I experience His love in ways I can't even describe. I then ask God to pour His love through me to my friends.

When I released the book *Cultivating Deeper Connections in a Lonely World*, I realized that many women needed a physical reminder of God's presence in their lives. I had a bracelet designed that is engraved with the words, "Never Alone." As women have purchased these bracelets, I can't tell you how many times I've heard that the bracelet is a tangible reminder that God is with them, no matter their circumstances. As they have felt more secure with God, they have formed deeper attachments with others.

In our quest for deeper attachment, it can be helpful to seek God together as friends. This does two things: First, it can deepen your experience of God's presence. Second, it deepens your attachment with your friends.

Here are a few suggestions for doing this:

Set aside a day to spend together seeking God. You might spend time outside or you could go to a retreat center or monastery. The key is to schedule the time and agree you're going to try to spend a day in prayer together.

Spend time worshiping together. Choose worship music that you both like to prompt your praise. As you listen, go back and forth praising God for all He has done.

Read Scripture out loud to each other. A friend and I recently did this. As we sat outside looking toward the mountains, we took turns reading Psalm 84. It's wonderful to hear Scripture from the voice of a dear friend.

Take turns sharing prayer requests, and spend time praying blessing over each other. I have loved doing this with friends. As you pray for each other and ask God to pour out His blessing on you both, your experience of God's love will grow deeper, and your bond will grow stronger.

Friend, I know that God wants you to experience deep attachment to both Him and others. He wants you to experience the fullness of His love and presence as well as the joy and love of close friendships. If it's been a while since you've truly felt God's love and enjoyed His presence, try spending a day in prayer with a friend with the above suggestions. See if it doesn't increase your experience of God's presence and deepen your bond with your friend.

Friendship Wisdom

Prioritize spending a day in prayer and worship with a friend. Set aside a day in your schedule and at the end of the day reflect on what you both experienced.

Pause and Reflect

How might feeling completely secure in God's love impact your friendships? As you think about the suggestions for how to experience God's presence in this chapter, which one resonates the most?

Prayer

Lord God, I long to experience Your presence in more tangible ways. I want to not just know in my head that You love me, I want to feel it to the depths of my soul. So often, Lord, I am distracted by all of the noise of our culture. I get wrapped up in busyness and forget that You are with me constantly. Teach me to enjoy Your presence daily, I pray. Show me what it looks like to live with a moment-by-moment awareness that You are with me. May I rest today in the fact that I am deeply loved by You. May I love my friends out of the overflow of a fully secure heart.

"A good friend is someone who shows empathy."

Amber Lia

Author, Health Coach

CHAPTER 9

Stop Over-Functioning

Walk in the way of insight.
PROVERBS 9:6

I have a confession: I am a recovering over-functioner! "Over-functioning is when you do for someone else what they can and should do for themselves."[1] It could also be defined as stepping in to take control. In addition to having secure boundaries, if we want strong friendships, some of us need to stop over-functioning.

Here's what this has looked like in my life. I value my friendships, and I love it when everybody gets along. When I have sensed friction between close friends of mine, I've been tempted to step in and try to fix the conflict. However, this is not a good idea. I'm not the HR director between my friends. I need to be able to trust them to work things out with each other.

Over-functioning happens often in friendships. For example, one friend is frustrated with how things are going in her marriage, and so another friend finds a counselor and sets up an appointment for her friend. That's not loving; that's over-functioning. If a friend wants counseling, she is fully capable of finding a counselor on her own and even calling to set up the appointment. If on the other hand your friend asks you for a recommendation, then you can suggest counseling options.

Over-functioning frequently happens in parenting and can negatively affect the friendship element in a marriage. Perhaps Mom doesn't like the way Dad is handling discipline with the kids, so she steps in and takes over to smooth things out with her child. Her intentions are good, but she ends up over-functioning. She becomes a Maternal Gatekeeper. However, often Dad might simply be doing things his own way, and in Mom's efforts to protect her child she chooses over-functioning. As a result, their friendship also suffers. Dad eventually gives up and assumes the role of an under-functioner. Parents are to work together as friends and teammates as they raise their kids.

Martha is a classic example. When Jesus visits Martha and her sister Mary, Martha is concerned about all the details. She's scurrying around preparing dinner, setting the table, and making sure that everything is in perfect order. Who can blame her? If Jesus were coming to my home, I would want dinner and the setting to be perfect too. However, while she's doing all the work, she is seething with resentment toward her sister, who hadn't gotten up from sitting at the feet of Jesus to help (Luke 10:38–42). I wonder, did Martha ask Mary for help before Jesus got there? Had she invited Mary to help her get everything ready? Or did she just do it all herself, but resented Mary for not thinking of helping her? So many questions. This I know—when we over-function in relationships, we end up resenting the person we are over-functioning for. What could Martha have done differently? She could have relaxed. She could have told Mary, let's sit with our friend for a while, and then let's work together to get lunch ready. Instead, she took on all the responsibility for preparing a meal but inwardly boiled with anger.

The pattern of over-functioning is all too common in friendships. Years ago, I knew a woman who helped a friend get her financial house in order. The problem was she never learned to say no. She continually bailed her friend out of debt and ended up resenting her. Eventually, the friendship imploded.

When we take on too much responsibility, we end up filled with resentment. Instead, we need to break the unhealthy cycle of over-functioning.

How Do We Break the Cycle?

I have discovered that there are three steps to break the cycle of over-functioning:

Ask the Holy Spirit to show you when you are over-functioning. The Holy Spirit is more than willing to search our hearts and show us where we need to grow. You might be over-functioning in your friendships. You might be over-functioning in your parenting journey or in your career. Ask the Holy Spirit to reveal your areas of taking over control and to make it crystal clear. The next step is to identify what's prompting the behavior.

Identify the fears or anxieties behind your behavior. Often, we believe, "If I don't do it, no one will." Or we might believe, "By doing this, I am loving well, and others will love and appreciate me more." Or, "If I don't do this, it won't be done correctly." I guarantee that if you stop over-functioning, someone else will pick up the slack. The irony is that by doing something that someone else can and should be doing, you won't experience more love. People may just take advantage of you. Additionally, you will be robbing them of the opportunity to grow in maturity. After you've asked the Holy Spirit to show you where you are over-functioning, and you've identified the fears and anxieties behind your behavior, it's time for the third most challenging step.

Surrender to God's control. Trusting God is really about relaxing in His sovereignty. I have found, as a former over-functioner, that I must often physically open my hands and reaffirm my trust in God's sovereign control. I then breathe deeply and remind myself that I can rest in His care. God doesn't need me to take over. Now, I have had to repeat this process many times. But gradually, I am learning that I truly can relax as I trust God to handle challenging situations.

Many of us have over-functioned for so long that breaking the cycle is going to take serious work. As you practice letting go, I guarantee you will experience far more peace, both in your soul and also in your relationships.

Friendship Wisdom

To stop over-functioning, learn to continually surrender to the control of the Holy Spirit. This will take time; often the act of surrender must happen continually. But gradually, you'll begin to relax and trust others to take care of their own issues.

Pause and Reflect

In which friendships are you most likely to over-function or take control? What fear triggers you to over-function?

Prayer

Oh, Lord Jesus, I realize my own tendencies to take control and over-function. Forgive me and cleanse me. I pray that You would bring quick conviction to my heart. Reveal the situations where I am most likely to take control. Show me the fears that are driving this behavior so that I can release those fears to You. I pray that through the power of Your Holy Spirit, You would enable me to relax and simply trust You.

CHAPTER 10

Let Go of Trying to Be the Expert

A chattering fool comes to ruin.
PROVERBS 10:8B

The prudent hold their tongues.
PROVERBS 10:19

Have you ever been around someone who continually tries to be the expert? I have, and it's annoying. "Experts" give unsolicited advice. They have a solution to every problem you have. They try to "fix" you, and they talk about what they've accomplished or learned. But they are perceived as chattering fools and end up losing their credibility.

A good rule of thumb for great friendships is to not give advice unless you're asked. Often, our love for a friend compels us to try to fix their problem. After all, we don't want them to feel pain. So, we offer our best wisdom: "You know what you should do?" Then we go on to tell them exactly what to do. The problem is that people don't want advice unless they've asked. Friends don't want you to fix their problems, they want support, empathy, and prayer.

The wise writer of Proverbs reminds us that a chattering fool comes to ruin. In my opinion, there's no faster way to become a fool than to give unsolicited advice. The wise friend holds their tongue and simply focuses on listening.

Wanting to help turns into our most persuasive argument for why our friend should follow our advice. Here's the thing: Most people's problems are complicated. If you feel you can fix their problem with a simple solution, that makes you come across as arrogant. When that happens, people may back away from the friendship. Who wants to be friends with someone who continually shows up as "the expert"?

This happens all the time with mothers of young children. A toddler is not sleeping through the night, and some well-meaning older friend dives in with, "Let me give you advice on sleep training." The mom of young kids is going to be annoyed and will likely put distance in the friendship.

I once had a friend give me all sorts of advice on making my speaking ministry more effective. The only problem? I hadn't asked, and my friend wasn't an expert on speaking. I stayed quiet but eventually backed up.

How Do We Stop Trying to Be the Expert?

Ask Jesus to heal the places of your heart where you initially experienced trauma. Where did the need to be the expert come from? A need to feel superior can stem from the trauma of being undervalued or not given a voice. At times we think of trauma as only horrific events from the past. But trauma can come from smaller childhood episodes where we felt we weren't seen or heard. Out of that place of pain rises a cavernous need to be perceived as the expert. Maybe it was being put on the spot by a teacher and fearing embarrassment if your answer wasn't good enough. Or, being called stupid or being chosen last for a team when you were a kid. Wherever your fear that you weren't enough began, ask Jesus to bring healing.

Focus on understanding. Often the need to give advice is quieted when we shift our attention to listening. Sometimes, when I'm tempted to give unsolicited advice, I put my hand over my mouth and try to understand the heart behind what my friend is sharing. Rather than coming up with a solution to offer, I can instead offer empathy.

Praise God that you don't need to be the expert. You don't need to know all the answers. God is the only one who truly is all-knowing. One of the lies of the enemy is that we fall victim to is that we need to know the answer. Most friends are not looking for an answer. They are looking for someone who will hear them and offer empathy. If your general personality is to strive to have all the answers, that's a great habit to ask God to change. It's okay not to be the expert. It's far better to show up as a learner in friendship.

Friendship Wisdom

Next time you're tempted to give unsolicited advice, close your mouth, maybe even put your hand over your mouth, and focus instead on offering empathy.

Pause and Reflect

When did you first feel like you needed to be an expert in some area? How has that impacted your friendships?

Prayer

Lord, teach me to have Your mind and to put on humility in my friendships. When I feel tempted to fix a problem or offer unsolicited advice, please, Holy Spirit, remind me to listen more empathetically. I don't want to be a chattering fool trying to solve other people's problems. Remind me that You are the One who is the problem solver. I can simply offer my listening ears and my understanding heart and that will be enough.

CHAPTER 11

Be Trustworthy, Keep Confidences

A gossip betrays a confidence,
But a trustworthy person keeps a secret.
PROVERBS 11:13

A gossip separates close friends.
PROVERBS 16:28

We became friends quickly, and I thought it was going to be a beautiful friendship. We shared our hearts, and I told the details of my story. However, over time, I discovered that my new friend had related those private details to another friend. I felt betrayed, and my trust eroded. I eventually realized that this was a pattern in my new acquaintance's life. She divulged "concerns" to others as prayer requests. At first glance, it felt godly. I mean, who doesn't need prayer? However, those concerns had often been told in confidence. A true and trustworthy friend will keep your secrets and stay far away from gossip.

Gradually, our friendship fell apart as I could no longer trust the person I thought was a mighty prayer warrior. I don't doubt that her intentions were good and that she truly loved prayer. The problem is that when you betray a confidence, it's hard to win back that trust. I could no longer offer my trust, and instead, I backed away from that relationship.

Solomon wrote that "a gossip separates close friends" (Prov. 16:28). There are a lot of misconceptions floating around about gossip. For example, some people think it's not gossip if it's true. That's incorrect. Gossip is talking behind someone's back and sharing information about a person that influences another's opinion of them, often negatively. Gossip can take the form of speculating about someone's motives and telling that information to another. Or it can look like breaking confidences and revealing confidential information about one person to another. If a friend shares something in confidence with you, hold that as a treasure and keep it private. Guarding secrets is something even childhood friends understand. (The only exception is when something illegal or dangerous is happening. Then go to a pastor, counselor, or the authorities.) The point is to honor the trust someone else has placed in you. Holding someone else's private information is sacred.

Now let me offer a caveat. At times, when you are struggling in a relationship with another person, you need the advice of a close and wise, trusted friend. However, be careful to seek advice and not digress into simply bashing or speaking negatively about the other person.

Paul reminds us in his letter to the believers at Ephesus that we are not to "let any unwholesome talk come out of your mouths, but only what is helpful for building others up according to their needs, that it may benefit those who listen" (Eph. 4:29). Good questions to ask ourselves are: "How will this information benefit the listener? Will it help or hurt the reputation of the person I am speaking about? Is it helpful to build another person up?"

Even as I write this, I realize I have also messed up in this area. Needing to vent, I have at times participated in gossip. I have had to ask the Holy Spirit to cleanse my heart and take over my mouth so that I only say what is beneficial to build up another. I want to be a trustworthy friend who not only keeps the private thoughts of another but who also doesn't engage in any gossip.

Many years ago, in 1872, Mary Ann Pietzker wrote the poem "Is it True? Is it Necessary? Is it Kind?" Those three questions should become gatekeepers for our mouths and our social media accounts! Too many friendships have been destroyed because, whether well-meaning or not, we have broken confidences and gossiped, and people's reputations have been torn down.

Next time you are tempted to share some "information" about another, ask yourself, Is this true? Is it necessary to share? Is it kind? How will this help the person's reputation? You might even ask yourself, how will this impact my relationship? If you're not sure what to say, stay quiet. It's better to be quiet than to blab too much information about another person.

Friendship Wisdom

Keep the trust of another by not disclosing what they deem confidential.

Pause and Reflect

Has anyone ever broken your confidence by sharing private information about you with another? How did that make you feel? What was the impact on your relationship? Taking the lesson learned from that situation, how can you be more discerning about what to share with others?

Prayer

Lord Jesus, I praise You that You are trustworthy in every situation. I long to be a trustworthy friend; so, Holy One, teach me to keep the confidences of others. Set a guard over my mouth so that I don't share with others information or stories that are not mine to share. I pray that You would help me take confidentiality seriously and that my friends would be able to trust me implicitly.

"A good friend is someone who you can tell anything to and who loves you unconditionally."

JUDY DUNAGAN

Author, Bible Teacher

CHAPTER 12

Be Affirming

Whoever refreshes others will be refreshed.
PROVERBS 11:25

During a particularly dark season in my life, having lunch or coffee with Margaret was a delight. She is extraordinary. Walking through church hurt, an extended family crisis, and cancer had left me flat-out exhausted. Yet, whenever I got together with Margaret, I left refreshed. She would say things like, "Becky, the Lord is using you. Notice how you press into Him, and He has gifted you with creativity." Or, "Becky, your Sunday dinners are so great! You are doing such a great job with your teen girls." Her uplifting words were like water to my parched soul. I grew up with a mom who was often critical. In the chaos of ministry life, the critics are plenty. But Margaret was different. She looked for the good in people and was generous with affirmation. During those challenging years, I would say to my husband, "Everybody needs one call or coffee with Margaret every day because she is so life-giving!" Can you imagine 1-800-dial Margaret to receive your daily affirmation for the day?

These many years later, I look back on my times with Margaret fondly. I learned much from her about how the human soul craves affirmation and how I can play a small role in encouraging someone with my words.

Here's the thing: Many in our world are discouraged. Angry critics abound, and on social media, the critics lob their opinions. I often wonder: How is this helping the condition of our souls? What if instead, we offered our words to the Lord and asked Him to help us encourage one other person every day? Our family members and friends would feel so much more valued.

One of the practices I love to encourage as a leadership coach is affirming each other. Every person logs in to feel competent, valued, and appreciated. When they feel those things, stronger bonds develop. As a result, they are more willing to go the extra mile for the company or a nonprofit.

Words of affirmation is identified as one of the five love languages in the bestselling book by Dr. Gary Chapman, *The 5 Love Languages.* Words of affirmation are apparently the most common of all the love languages. I wonder if, beyond each of us having primary ways we feel loved, that universally everyone needs such words. When we affirm others with our words, our connection automatically grows, and our friendship deepens.

The apostle Paul understood this. When he wrote to the believers living in Philippi, he affirmed their holiness, their love, and their partnership in the gospel. He wrote that he longed for them, he had them in his heart, and he was confident in them (Phil. 1:1–8). What a beautiful example of words of affirmation.

Let me ask you:

How would friendships flourish if you told your friends how they inspire you?

What if you told your friends you love how radiant they are or how joyful they are?

How would friendship grow at work if you told your coworker that their work ethic is so encouraging to you?

What if you told a friend that you admire their parenting style?

In a world where criticism abounds, every person is longing to be valued. When you start using words of affirmation, your friendships are sure to thrive. You can count on it! How do we do this in practical ways?

Be honest. When you affirm others, be genuine. People can read through flattery. The writer of Proverbs says that "a flattering mouth works ruin" (Prov. 26:28). Flattery is shallow, insincere praise. That's not what we mean by affirming others. When we affirm others, we verbally call attention to their good qualities. We don't exaggerate. We don't manipulate. We verbally express our appreciation to that person. For example, you might affirm your friend's patience or gentleness in their parenting. You might notice and appreciate how they demonstrate kindness to others or how they always seem to know the right thing to say.

Be creative. Deliver flowers to a friend and attach a note that tells them, "I'm just thinking about how inspired I am by you!" Or send a card that expresses how much you admire their prayer life and appreciate their friendship. Another creative way to affirm your friends is to brag about them in front of other friends. For example, when you're introducing them, you might say, "This is my friend Lisa, and she is amazing at balancing her work and business life.' Or, "This is my friend Tonda, and she is one of the most creative people I have ever met."

Be intentional. Think through your list of friends. Who might need a word of encouragement in this season? Notice the details of what makes your friend so wonderful. Send a card and write out specific qualities you appreciate about them. Spend time considering what you love about your friends. Then perhaps set a goal to send one affirming text message per day. Keep track of who you send the text messages to so that all your friends receive at least one. If you notice in your home that you are being critical of a family member, commit to the Lord to offer a word of affirmation every day for the next thirty days. I'm guessing your loved one will feel more connected.

Be specific. The more specific you are, the greater the impact of your affirmation. Take time to consider what specifically you are thankful for in your friendship. What do you love and appreciate about each friend? Then use your words to affirm them. For example, you might say to your friend, "I am grateful because you listen intentionally when I'm sharing my heart. Thank you."

Friendship Wisdom

Buy a special card for a friend today. Inside, express how grateful you are for their friendship and list five things you love about them. Then be sure to actually mail the card!

Pause and Reflect

Think through one of your friendships. How might you grow closer to each of those people if you started using words of affirmation more frequently?

Prayer

Lord God, I thank You that affirmation was Your idea. Thank You for the words of the apostle Paul, who wrote to the believers in Philippi: I thank God every time I remember you. He affirmed them because they had been great partners to him, and he felt confident that God was going to continue a good work in them. Holy One, help me to follow Paul's example and use my words to affirm my friends. Help me to remember that my words can be used to refresh weary hearts. Today, Lord, I give You my mouth. Lead me to situations where I can use my words to affirm others.

"A good friend celebrates your wins but also sits with you in your losses."

Laura Acuna

Author, Speaker, Life Coach

CHAPTER 13

Be Willing to Accept Advice

The wise listen to advice.
PROVERBS 12:15

Wisdom is found in those who take advice.
PROVERBS 13:10

We sat at dinner in a restaurant in upstate New York. As the director of women's ministries in my church, I had brought Linda Dillow in to speak at our weekend event. We should have been talking through the schedule of the event and all the details, but my mind was far away. I knew I wanted to write a book, so when Linda asked about my dreams as a ministry worker, I shared that dream. As Linda talked about her own writing journey, I knew what I wanted: to journey with this wise woman at my side. As the writer of Proverbs wrote, "Walk with the wise and become wise" (Prov. 13:20). So, leaning across the table, I boldly asked, "Will you mentor me?" Linda thought for a moment and then said yes. She lived in a different state in an entirely different part of the country. Yet, she agreed. That conversation began a mentoring friendship that has lasted over twenty years.

At different points in our relationship, Linda has given me advice. She has earned the right because she's invested so much in my life. She advised counseling for the childhood sexual abuse I had never dealt with. She recommended a well-known editor to get my first proposal in shape. She guided me in how to grow deeper in my relationship with God and my husband. I realized quickly that if I was going to grow in wisdom, I needed to be willing to listen to advice.

Today, Linda and I are still close friends. Our relationship is a bit different now, but as I look back, I am so thankful that I asked Linda to mentor me. I'm thankful that I was willing to listen to advice. Otherwise, I would not be where I am today in my life and ministry.

Now, you might be wondering, "If I am being mentored, is it wise to do everything according to the advice I receive?" I always took any advice that Linda gave me back to the Lord for confirmation. If I sensed that He wanted something different, I did what I felt He was asking me to do.

All that said, I have noticed in our current culture that there is resistance to receiving any kind of advice. Many feel they are the experts, and as such, they feel they don't need advice. I already explained how it's not advisable to give unwarranted advice. However, if you are in a close relationship with someone and you're not willing to receive advice, there might be an arrogance problem. Further, you likely won't grow in wisdom.

Beyond mentoring relationships, I have been blessed with many wise friends who know me well. These are friends who seek the Lord's wisdom first in their lives. In our friendship, there have been times when they've given me advice and times when I've given them advice. I think of Gayle, who I met as she walked through breast cancer. We had that in common, and I felt an almost instant connection with her. At times, Gayle has given me business advice for my coaching practice. There have been times when I have given Gayle advice. Neither of us gets frustrated or offended because the depth of our relationship makes it feel safe. Another friend, Keri, has given me advice on which apps I need and which to ignore. Maybe you don't need advice about apps, but I sure do! Another friend has given me advice on how to frame pictures economically and professionally. I need all these friends. That is the beauty of walking through life with wise friends. You might need advice on a problem with your teen or with an investment you're thinking of making. Maybe you need advice on what to serve at a dinner party you're hosting. Think through your friends. Who might be able to come alongside you with some good tips?

Beyond the common life issues there are times when we are trying to make a large decision. Our friends, who know us well, can often serve as sounding boards and discerning listeners. As we make ourselves vulnerable and ask for their advice when we feel stuck, their input can be invaluable. Part of a healthy friendship is a trust bond that allows vulnerability and comfortability with asking for feedback. Often discernment comes in a group context.

During one season in our marriage, Steve and I were trying to decide about a move across the country to serve in a new ministry. We felt torn over the options before us, and so after we prayed as a couple, we sought the counsel of several godly friends. They agreed to pray and gave us some wise advice on how to determine if God was in the move. Having their wisdom surround us felt like a shield of protection as we were about to take what we considered to be a scary leap of faith. They aided us in the discernment process.

You might not be wrestling with a move across the country but perhaps you are wrestling with other decisions. Consider your friends. Which do you consider wise? Seek them out; make yourself vulnerable. Ask for their advice. You don't have to follow their advice but listen and then go back to the Lord. Seek His heart. See if He speaks anything through the whisper of His Spirit or through His Word. Never take advice that is contrary to the Word of God. If the counsel of your friend lines up with God's Word and your spirit feels peace that aligns with the Holy Spirit, take that advice to heart.

Our wise friends can build a wall of protection around us, but only if we're willing to lean into them. I wonder how many unwise decisions could be avoided if we would learn to humble ourselves and listen to the advice of the wise.

Friendship Wisdom

Be willing to listen and consider advice from wise and godly friends.

Pause and Reflect

What makes you resistant to receiving or even considering advice from others? What was your response internally to this chapter? What do you feel like God is speaking to you?

Prayer

Lord, I find myself often bristling when others give me advice. At the end of the day, I want to please You alone. However, I recognize that You have put godly and wise people around me. Show me what it looks like to lean into them and seek wise counsel. Holy Spirit, I ask You to reshape my heart toward humility. Bring my will into alignment with Yours. I pray that You would grant me the grace of a teachable spirit. Help me not to view myself as the expert in all things, but rather to recognize that there are areas in my life where I need the wise counsel of others.

"A good friend asks meaningful questions to help you celebrate, mourn, grow, reflect, dream, worship, grapple with life, and laugh."

Dr. Heather Holleman

Author, Associate Professor of English, Pennsylvania State University

CHAPTER 14

Invest in Friendships in Your Family

The wise woman builds her house, but with her own hands, the foolish one tears hers down.

PROVERBS 14:1

I had two of my little granddaughters over. We were going to enjoy a day of crafts and fun, giggles and snuggles. However, as often happens with siblings, an argument broke out and tears ensued between the sisters. After I comforted each one, I told them, "Hey, you know what? You guys are going to be friends forever because you're sisters." Then I went on to say, "You know what that makes you? Fristers!" (Friends + sisters = Fristers!) They both thought that was the funniest word, and giggles replaced tears. There is nothing quite as sweet as sisters getting along. However, in many families, fighting is the norm.

Dysfunction abounds. I have friends whose kids won't talk with them. I know families where siblings are enemies. Family systems are a whole thing, right? Sometimes, the dysfunction is so great that it is no longer safe to be in close relationship with your family members. I get that. However, where it's possible, as it depends on you, I believe God wants us to try to cultivate friendships within our families.

The wise woman tries to cultivate emotionally healthy friendships within her family. In the Bible, family referred to your extended family going back three or four generations. It's important to note that in Proverbs 14:1, Solomon is not encouraging a woman to build a physical house. He's referring to her family life. God's heart for the family is that each person has a place to belong and feel loved. Obviously, that has gone awry in our culture. However, learning to cultivate friendship within your family system is a very biblical idea.

Remember Joseph? Of course you do. He was his daddy's favorite and had dreams of having power over his brothers. Perhaps, at seventeen, he lacked the wisdom to keep those dreams to himself. Instead, he told his brothers that someday they would all bow down to him. What could go wrong with a statement like that? Long story short, his brothers—who already hated him because of their father's love for Joseph—got sick of his dreams and sold him to slave traders. Many years later, Joseph rose to the top leadership in Egypt. When famine hit and his brothers arrived begging for food, Joseph had the perfect opportunity to seek revenge because they no longer recognized him. But he eventually revealed who he was. Then he did something extraordinary. Joseph invited his brothers to come close. He told them not to be angry with themselves for selling him off because God had a plan to save them (Gen. 45:4–5).

I am intrigued by this conversation. The brothers had not apologized. Yet, Joseph invited them close and offered friendship. By doing so, he broke the pattern of lying and bitterness that had crippled his family. I believe there is a lesson on family life tucked within these verses.

Every family has its fair share of turmoil. However, part of God's plan for the family is that it's a place where we can practice forgiveness and grace. You don't have to be "besties" with your brothers or sisters or cousins, but I do believe, as much as it depends on you, that you should try to cultivate friendship within your family. What does this look like?

Take an honest look at the dysfunction in your family. Pete Scazzero recommends doing a genogram to trace the unhealthy or sinful patterns in your family. This is a wise idea for several reasons. For example, often, if we don't take a truthful look at our family's dysfunction, we will repeat the pattern. Scazzero writes, "Jesus may be in your heart, but Grandpa is in your bones."[1]

Ask the Holy Spirit to empower you to break unhealthy cycles. When we uncover all the dysfunction in our families, the first impulse for many is to run! We want to get away from the craziness. God, however, invites us to break the cycle. In Joseph's case, he brings his brothers to him. Joseph might have been happy just being in power and staying far away from his family, but that was not God's plan. God wanted Joseph to break the cycle and reconnect.

Offer forgiveness and friendship. God invited Joseph to offer forgiveness and friendship to the very brothers who had sold him into slavery. He offers you the same invitation. At times it is not possible to offer friendship because it's dangerous to you. But most often, God's plan is reconciliation.

So many families are splintered. Cutting people off is becoming the norm. But that is not God's plan. He wrote through Solomon that the wise woman builds her house—her family. Stay connected. Break the cycle of dysfunction. Offer forgiveness and friendship within your family system. I know it's hard, but the Holy Spirit is more than able to empower you.

Friendship Wisdom

Offer forgiveness and friendship within your immediate and extended family.

Pause and Reflect

In your family, how have you been wounded? How might offering forgiveness and friendship within the family help bring healing?

Prayer

Lord God, family is so important, and yet at times, I find that I clash with different members of my family. I pray that You would show me how to find healing from childhood wounds. Show me, I pray, what it looks like to love my family members as You do. I pray that I would take the bold step to cultivate friendships within my extended family system that reflect Your heart. Holy Spirit, forgive through me I pray. May my life extend Your grace.

CHAPTER 15

Pursue Gentleness, Even in Conflict

A gentle answer turns away wrath,
but a harsh word stirs up anger.
PROVERBS 15:1

I watched in utter disbelief as one woman blew up at the other. I was twenty-four at the time and had perhaps unrealistic expectations of those who consider themselves ministry leaders. As the scene unfolded, my only thought left was, "I have to get out of here!" Steve and I were leading a spiritual life conference overseas. The two women were supposedly friends, but what I witnessed felt closer to hatred. Strong opinions were expressed with shouting, crying, and stomping out of the room. We were supposed to be praying, but what ensued was not prayer.

Later that night, I lay in bed reflecting. I remember praying something like, "Lord, this is nuts! Get us out of this country please!" God didn't answer that prayer according to my wishes, but as I watched over the next week or so, I learned a lot about how not to handle conflict.

In our cancel culture, it is more important than ever that we as followers of Christ learn how to handle conflict and disagreements in a way that honors our faith.

Conflict is going to be a part of every relationship. I wish it wasn't true. But it is. I hate conflict and haven't always handled it well. My natural tendency is to duck and take cover or conversely to talk faster hoping the conflict will end sooner. Neither of those strategies has been helpful. Through the years, I've grown in my communication skills. I've invested in coaching and have learned how to navigate conflict a bit more effectively.

Gentleness is God's desire for us even when we are actively engaged in disagreements or conflict. Solomon wrote wisely that, "A gentle answer turns away wrath" (Prov. 15:1). In other words, while gentleness diffuses anger, retorts stir up more fire in the conflict.

Two women in the church in Philippi were also having trouble getting along, and Paul wrote to the church asking that they come alongside the women and help them work out their differences (Phil. 4:1–3). Then Paul went on a few verses later to say, "Let your gentleness be evident to all" (v. 5). Gentleness is evidence of the Holy Spirit's work in our lives. Even in conflict, we must demonstrate the fruit of the Spirit (Gal. 5:22).

Too often, I have seen leaders sacrifice their credibility because they've lost their tempers. I've seen friendships destroyed because one friend blew up at another, and I have seen marriages crumble because one partner or the other cannot control their temper!

Through the years, I have watched friends and coworkers handle conflict, and I've noticed a few unhealthy patterns. Now, to be honest, I have handled conflict in some unhealthy ways. However, I want to encourage us to mature to the point where we can navigate conflict with godliness.

Unhealthy Ways to Handle Conflict

Exploding in anger. Explosive anger is never a good idea. You may feel powerful in the moment, but you forfeit your credibility. Self-control is one of the fruits of the Spirit, and we must continue to ask the Holy Spirit to create self-control in us. When we shout or yell at another person, it's a sign that the Holy Spirit is not in control of our hearts.

Ghosting. This is where you hate conflict, so you simply back away and never deal with the problem authentically. You simply stop answering the person because you don't want to deal with the real issues. As a result, you lose the friendship.

Ignoring the issues, while seething with resentment. This is a big temptation for those of us who love peace. We don't want to rock the boat, so we ignore the issues. However, the whole time we're ignoring we're seething with resentment. It would be so much better to bring the issues out in the open and to navigate the conversation with gentleness.

Healthy and Godly Ways to Navigate Conflict

First, pause and pray. Now it's not always convenient to bow your head and pray. But what you can do is pause your talking and pray internally for the Holy Spirit to calm your heart. Ask Him very specifically to take over your mouth so that you don't say something you will regret later.

Focus on listening more than talking. This is counterintuitive. When in conflict, we want to talk and defend ourselves. However, if we stop talking and listen and allow the other person to finish dumping, it gives our bodies, souls, and spirits a few moments to calm down. As we focus on understanding what the other person is saying, we will be calmer in the conflict and less likely to forfeit our gentleness. Great advice is "Everyone should be quick to listen, slow to speak and slow to become angry" (James 1:19b). When we switch our focus to listening rather than planning our next rebuttal, we allow the other person to feel heard and valued. As a result, the conflict defuses rather than intensifying.

Fix and repair quickly. Friendships are precious, so don't let the conflict go on unresolved. Where you can take responsibility, take it. Apologize where you can. Offer understanding of the other person's perspective and be quick to repair whatever damage has been done. This is why Scripture instructs us not to let the sun go down on our wrath (Eph. 4:26). I have noticed that some hang on to feeling hurt or angry long after the argument has been resolved. Life is too short to let bitterness fester. Resolve things quickly and reaffirm that the friendship is important.

Relationships are precious, and yes, there will be conflict. However, when you navigate conflict with gentle wisdom, the result is a stronger connection.

Friendship Wisdom

Cultivate gentleness in your life.

Pause and Reflect

What is your go-to method for handling conflict? Do others perceive you as gentle? Ask three people close to you how you are doing in the gentleness department.

Prayer

Holy Spirit, gentleness is a fruit of a life filled with You. Fill me, I pray today, so that I am known for demonstrating gentleness even when I engage in conflict. Lord, this is a tough skill to learn. Only You can form this within me. I pray that You would bring my attitude and heart into perfect alignment with Yours in this area. Help me not to use my natural tendencies or personality traits as an excuse. Instead, help me to lean into Your perfection more and more.

CHAPTER 16

Nurture Patience

Better a patent person than a warrior,
one with self-control than one who takes a city.

PROVERBS 16:32

My husband and I, and several of our kids, were sitting just outside a fast-food restaurant in a mall in California. People were exiting the restaurant, completely annoyed. Every single person came out and threw their drink in the trash. None of them had food, only a large drink, which they disgustedly tossed. We were curious. After about thirty minutes, we asked people what was happening. The answer was that no matter what they ordered, the restaurant gave them a large Sprite. Our son wasn't sure that was really true, so he went inside and ordered a double burger, fries, and a Coke. Sure enough, when he went to pick up his order, there was only a large Sprite. As a family, we still laugh about that scenario today and often wonder if it was some type of hidden camera reality TV show. We'll never know. All we do know is that people were sure annoyed, and some were downright angry.

Lately, I've noticed that in our culture, people become easily annoyed. Don't get me wrong, a restaurant messing up your order is a little annoying. However, it seems that people get annoyed over anything that doesn't fit their opinion or inconveniences them. Have you noticed that?

Patience is a virtue that is affirmed all through the Scriptures. Sometimes, it's in reference to waiting, but often it's in regard to controlling how annoyed we get with people. Solomon wrote, "better is a patient person than a warrior" (Prov. 16:32). The apostle Paul, when describing love, states that "it is not easily angered" (1 Cor. 13:5). Some translations state it is not easily annoyed, or provoked, or irritable. If we want strong relationships and good friends, we need to be people who are not easily annoyed. After all, our faith invites us to be transformed into the image of Christ.

God's very nature is patient. Consistently through the Old and New Testament, we see the patience of God. The psalmist writes, "the Lord is compassionate and gracious, slow to anger, abounding in love" (Ps. 103:8). Did you catch that? God is slow to anger. He's not easily annoyed. In the New Testament, Paul describes the evidence that the Holy Spirit is present in our lives by those who have "love, joy, peace, forbearance" (better known as "patience") (Gal. 5:22). God's priority in your life and mine is that we be transformed into the image of His Son, Jesus Christ. And that means we will reflect God's patience in our friendships.

Practical Ways Patience Plays Out in Friendship

Realize it takes time to develop long-term friendships. Don't dive into a friendship and assume that person is going to be your "bestie" for years to come. Long-term friendships take time to develop. Go slow and pray as you go that the Lord will give you insight into your friend's heart.

Be slow to get angry or annoyed. Again, patience means you're not going to be easily offended or annoyed. When I'm tempted to feel annoyed with a friend, I ask myself, "Is this worth feeling negatively toward her?" Often, the cause of my annoyance is some silly thing that

I need to overlook. This is particularly true in the realm of friendship in marriage. I want to be a good friend to my husband, and that means I must commit to overlooking and letting go of the things that annoy me. "The one who is patient calms a quarrel" (Prov. 15:18).

Keep a good attitude when waiting or being inconvenienced. Wrapped up in our quest for patience is also the concept of waiting. How patient are you when a friend is running late? How patient are you when emergencies arise and your plans are interrupted? In strong, healthy friendships, we are fine being inconvenienced because we love each other. We are patient when interrupted and gracious when inconvenienced. A good reflective question is, what is underneath your feelings of being impatient? Do you feel disrespected? Do you feel nervous about being late for the next appointment? Pausing and asking yourself about the *why* behind the feelings of annoyance can be helpful.

Demonstrate a willingness to overlook offenses. At some point, you will feel offended by a friend. Maybe you will feel overlooked or as though you're putting more effort into the relationship. Maybe your friend will point out something that you did that they believed was wrong, or maybe they'll give unsolicited advice. No matter what they do, you have a choice. You can take offense and back up, or you can choose to overlook the matter and move on with your friendship. Proverbs teaches us that "whoever would foster love covers over an offense, but whoever repeats the matter separates close friends" (Prov. 17:9). When we cover an offense, it doesn't mean we sweep matters under the carpet. There will be things in a healthy friendship that you may need to address. However, we cover those offenses with grace and forgiveness.

Cultivate flexibility through changing seasons. Our friendships will change from season to season. During some seasons, friends have more time for each other than others. When the pressure is building and your friend is experiencing stress at work, they will likely have less time to get together. Friends who have school-age kids in sports, music, or other activities might have a full schedule and limited time. In the later years, friends might become forgetful or experience significant health challenges. Part of being patient is being flexible. Offer others the gift of understanding when seasons and circumstances change.

If we want strong life-giving friendships, we must, in the words of Paul, clothe ourselves in patience (Col. 3:12). As you grow in your patience, your friendships will grow deeper and richer. Likely, if you offer others patience, they'll offer you patience in return.

Friendship Wisdom

Cultivate patience in all areas of life so that it spills easily into your friendships.

Pause and Reflect

On a scale of 1 to 10, 1 being the least and 10 being the greatest, how would you rate your patience? What annoys you most easily? What does it look like to be patient in those circumstances?

Prayer

Lord Jesus, I feel like I have so much further to grow in patience. I recognize that I become agitated when I am inconvenienced. Oh, Lord, I long to be like You! Holy One, fill me, I pray. When I am tempted to get easily annoyed or impatient, quiet my heart. Help me to be still and to recognize that You are at work. Show me what it looks like to cultivate patience today.

CHAPTER 17

Laugh Together

A cheerful heart is good medicine.
PROVERBS 17:22

My friend Judy and I have had some amazing moments together. One time when I was living in Denver and she was living in Colorado Springs, we scheduled lunch together. We were going to meet at California Pizza Kitchen. It was one of our favorites. However, as I sat in the restaurant waiting, Judy didn't show up. I finally called, and that's when it hit us; we never clarified which CPK we were going to meet at. Both of us busted up laughing at our like-minded airheadedness (is that a word?). We still laugh about that to this day.

A friend once told me about a time when she was praying over people at a conference. The only problem? She had gum in her mouth, which fell out and got stuck in the hair of the woman she was praying over. Horrified, she just kept praying and praying and slowly worked the gum out of the woman's hair, popped it back in her mouth, and then said, amen! We laughed so hard at that story that I almost wet my pants. Note to self, don't chew gum while praying over people!

Another time, Steve and I were seated in a restaurant with our friends Carol and Gene. We were all laughing so hard, I thought for sure the wait staff would kick us out. I left that restaurant so refreshed!

Moments of laughter with my friends have been so fun and special. My theory is that life is too short not to laugh. Never underestimate the power of a good, hearty belly laugh! Laughter lightens our souls and allows joy to flow once again. And do you know what? It's good for your health as well.

According to the Mayo Clinic, laughter reduces stress, releases endorphins, increases your intake of oxygen, and stimulates your heart, lungs, and muscles. It also seems to improve your immune system, relieve pain, and improve your mental attitude.[1] Lest you think your Christian walk is to be all serious, the Bible also recommends laughter.

In the book of Ecclesiastes, Solomon wrote that there is "a time to weep and a time to laugh" (Eccl. 3:4). That principle holds true in our friendships. At times our friends need us to weep with them, but at other delightful moments, they need us to laugh with them. Laughter is good medicine for our friendships.

The psalmist describes the deep joy for the people of God when they were freed from exile and says that their "mouths were filled with laughter" (Ps. 126:2). Even Jesus had a sense of humor.

We imagine Jesus all serious, but I don't think that's the case. His humor is evident in the parables He told. Take, for instance, the parable of the mustard seed (Matt. 13:31–32). To see the humor in this parable, you need to understand that it was illegal for the Israelites to plant mustard seed because the plants were so messy that they would grow and take over an entire property. So, when Jesus said His kingdom was like a mustard seed, I imagine the people in the crowd were busting up with laughter. Jesus was a master communicator and just like many who teach today He used humor often to engage His listeners.

If you want to be a better friend, keep a sense of humor. Laughter reduces stress and builds connection, helps communication, and builds memories with friends. In light of the benefits, be intentional!

Be Intentional to Laugh with Friends

Learn to laugh at yourself and your embarrassing moments. We tend to take ourselves too seriously. Instead, what if we learned to be a little more lighthearted? When you do something embarrassing, like we all do, just have a good giggle. It will increase your resilience as a person, and you won't tend to hide just because you're embarrassed.

Be intentional about looking for humor every day. Some of our grandkids are in the season where they are learning to tell jokes. One joke we heard last night from one of our grandsons was, "Why is it so hot in the stadium after the big game?" We of course asked why? The answer was, "Because all the fans were gone." We had a good laugh together. One of the questions I like to ask my grands when they get home from school is, "What happened in school today that was funny?"

Play games that encourage laughter. Games such as Balderdash, Pictionary, or Charades can all encourage laughter among friends. There are many games that encourage laughter, so go on a hunt or create your own. Here's what I know: Looking for moments to laugh will build your connections and make you a more positive person and a better friend.

Ask God to restore your sense of joy. Often, there are hard seasons that might stretch on for months on end. Grieve and be authentic, but also ask God to restore your joy. Ask Him for specific moments of laughter in your grief. He wants to put laughter back in your mouth and delights to see you experience joy.

Friendship Wisdom

Laugh with your people.

Pause and Reflect

When was the last time you laughed hysterically with friends or family? How did you feel after?

Pray

Lord, I praise You that You have a sense of humor. The psalmist wrote about our mouths being filled with laughter and songs of joy (Ps. 126:2). Thank You for the gift of laughter! Oh, how we need a good belly laugh from time to time. I realize at times I have taken myself too seriously. Teach me the freedom of unrestrained laughter. Fill me with a sense of humor, and lead me to friends who also enjoy humor. When I am with my friends, fill our moments with joy and laughter as well as with serious conversations.

"A good friend is a good listener who cares about me, someone who finds the same things funny."

ARLENE PELLICANE

Author, Podcast Host, Speaker

CHAPTER 18

Create a Circle of Loyalty

A friend loves at all times.
PROVERBS 17:17

Karen, Dorothy, Mary Ann, Laurie, and Sharon have been friends for years. I met Karen, Dorothy, and Mary Ann about twenty-five years ago and have stayed in touch via Facebook. Though I didn't know Laurie or Sharon then, I knew they were all close friends. Recently, I had the opportunity to reconnect with Karen when I was out of state at a speaking event. Karen described her beautiful long-term friendship as part of the circle of five. All of them were raising kids when they met. Though Karen and her husband moved away because they were transferred for work, all of the women and their husbands were committed to keeping their circle of friendship alive.

Through the years, though moves have separated, kids have grown, and life has changed, their friendship has remained strong. I asked Karen what she felt was the secret to their long-term friendship. She said staying intentional about seeing one another but also being committed to honesty. These women view themselves as sisters in Christ and support each other, sharing their burdens and joys. They continue to gather and travel on trips together with their husbands and are faithful in their prayers for one another. Their loyal circle has provided beautiful stability for each of them through the years.

As I sat in a coffee shop with Karen, she told me how in just a few short weeks she would be travelling north to visit her friends once again. I left the coffee shop that day inspired and encouraged! Nothing beats a circle of loyal friends!

Loyalty is one of the most beautiful qualities I can think of in friendship. A loyal friend will ugly cry with you, encourage you when you feel like quitting, pray for you when life is hard, and stick by you even when you don't have your act together. They are steadfast and committed. They provide a safe place of belonging.

Some friends will be loyal for a lifetime, like Karen, Dorothy, Mary Ann, Laurie, and Sharon. Other friends are loyal for a season, but those seasons may change. Friends move away, or life circumstances dictate that they are no longer as available as they once were. I recently heard the analogy of a bus: There are friends on the bus who are near the front; they are dependable and close to your heart. In different seasons, some on the bus change seats, some get off and remain casual friends, some move closer to the front. This is the natural movement of life. I love that analogy because seasons of friendships ebb and flow.

When you create a circle of loyal friends, you create a community of belonging. Loyalty in friendships reduces stress levels and provides support in the challenging seasons. It increases your happiness and well-being. And it strengthens your trust muscles.

Assuming that's all true, what does it look like to be a loyal friend through life's ups and downs?

How to Be a Loyal Friend

Take initiative. If you want loyal friends, you must be willing to take the initiative. Make the phone call. Invite your friend to lunch. Send a card. Spend the money on a flight to visit a friend who lives out of state. Friendships must be reciprocal. If your friend always reaches out to you but you don't put the effort into reaching out to her, your friendship won't be able to sustain the years.

Be trustworthy and reliable. If you want to be a loyal friend, you need to show up. When crisis hits, or when your friend is feeling discouraged, show up. Be available to listen, to comfort, and to support. Seek to be a friend that others can count on. One who is consistent. Now, to clarify, this doesn't mean you compromise your boundaries, but it does mean you send the message that you are in the friendship for the long haul.

Stand by your friend when life falls apart. In all of our lives, there will be moments when life is hard and grief hits like a tsunami. There have been seasons in my life when friends' lives have been exceedingly challenging, and I regret to say that I was busy. I was probably doing good things. Even important things. All that aside, I have regrets for not showing up as intentionally as I should have. Don't make the same mistake. Instead, when your friend's life falls apart, be intentional in offering your comforting presence. You don't need to worry about saying the right thing. Just offer yourself and your tears.

All of us need a community of loyal friends who will surround us through thick and thin. If you want those types of friends, you must seek to *be* that loyal friend.

Friendship Wisdom

Be the faithful, loyal friend you want to have.

Pause and Reflect

Who have been your most loyal friends? As you think through those friendships what have been some of the keys to keeping those friends close? What can you do this week to thank them for their loyalty in your life?

Pray

Lord Jesus, You are the most loyal friend I will ever have! You are the friend who sticks closer than a brother. Your Word teaches me that You will never leave me nor forsake me. Instead, Your presence is constant in my life, and Your prayers for me are continual. I praise You, Lord, for Your faithfulness. Align my heart with Yours so that I might be that loyal friend to others.

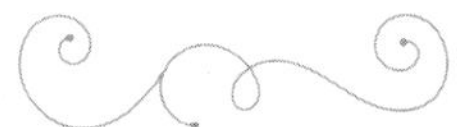

"A good friend is someone who
Holds your hand in the good and hard times.
She rejoices with you,
but also is willing to sit and weep with you when life falls apart."

Linda Dillow
Bestselling Author

CHAPTER 19

Listen More Than You Talk

To answer before listening—
that is folly and shame.
PROVERBS 18:13

I am a person who appreciates coffee and great conversations with friends. However, I remember a time years ago when I went out for coffee with a person who wanted to be friends; they never came up for air. It was a monologue with me trying to be a good listener but ending up exhausted. I was reluctant to get together with that person again. If you want to be a great friend, you must learn to listen.

I asked readers on social media what they valued in friendship. In other words, how would they describe a good friend? Many of the answers I received were about listening.

We live in a culture where many feel emboldened to air their opinions. The wise man Solomon made this profound statement, "Fools find no pleasure in understanding but delight in airing their own opinions" (Prov. 18:2). Wowza! That verse gives us pause for today, doesn't it? Would your friends describe you as a good listener? Do they view you as someone who seeks to understand and empathize with their feelings? Or do they view you as a person who wants to monopolize the conversation?

Early in our marriage, my husband and I entertained a well-known evangelist from our area. This gentleman had called my husband, Steve, to ask if he could preach at our tiny church. Because we were young and a bit nervous, we invited another couple who were friends to join us for the guest preacher's sermon. After the service, the evangelist, his wife, and our friends gathered in our home. The evangelist immediately started talking all about himself and his ministry. He began every sentence with, "As you know, I'll be speaking in Madison Square Garden" and "As you know *this*," and "As you know *that*."

After a while, our friend, Bob, looked the evangelist in the eye and said, "You know what? I never even heard of you before today!" The evangelist's wife jumped to her husband's defense: "How dare you talk to my husband that way!" The tension in the room was more than I could handle, so I quietly got up to make coffee. The two gentlemen went out on our porch to talk things over. My young husband was a nervous wreck, fearing they would get into a fist fight. Thankfully, that did not happen. However, Bob said to the man, "You never asked me one question about who I am or what I do. All you wanted to do was talk about yourself." The evangelist, to his credit, apologized. After everyone left that night, Steve and I went to bed exhausted, and both of us had headaches. However, looking back now, we both laugh. What a profound lesson. If you want friends, learn to listen more than you talk, especially about yourself!

What Does It Look Like to Listen Well in Friendship?

There are four principles to listening well. We'll use the word LEAD as an acrostic to help you remember.

L – Lean in and look people in the eye. This seems like such a simple principle. However, I am shocked by the number of people who are in conversation while they are scrolling on their phones. For people to feel loved by you, they have to *feel* heard. Often, I've heard the excuse, "But I am listening." Meanwhile, they are absorbed in something else. We're not talking about hearing. We're talking about listening, which makes the other person feel heard. Next time you're out with a friend, put away your phone. Lean in and look at your friend while they talk.

E – Empathize. Empathy says, "Your feelings make sense to me!" Your friends want to know that their feelings make sense to you. This is what Paul meant when he wrote, "Rejoice with those who rejoice; mourn with those who mourn" (Rom. 12:15). I have written before about what happens in our brains when someone empathizes with us: "God hard-wired your brain to empathize with others because it is mutually beneficial for both the person offering empathy and the person receiving empathy. Scientific research has uncovered 'mirror neurons', which react to emotions expressed by others and reproduce them."[1] Friend, we were wired to connect with others using empathy. The more you empathize, the more connected you and your friend will feel.

A – Ask questions. Such a simple practice but yet so profound. When you ask questions, you show that you are interested. When I started dating Steve, one of the first things I noticed was how great he was at asking questions. I felt his desire to know me. The same principle holds true in your friendships. Cultivate curiosity and ask your friend questions.

Recently, our grandson Josh joined a new soccer team. At the end of the practice, the coach went one by one through the players and asked them what they knew about Josh. If they didn't know anything, they had to drop and do a plank. I love that! We're all a bit guilty of "not knowing" from time to time. The temptation is to be self-focused rather than other-focused. What if, instead, we became master question askers who intentionally sought to know our friends better? We would be wise friends who follow the advice of Solomon when he wrote, "The purposes of a person's heart are deep waters, but one who has insight draws them out" (Prov. 20:5). The only way to truly understand your friend's heart is to learn to draw out their feelings.

D – Don't try to fix it. What do I mean? At times, when a friend shares a problem or concern, the first thing that pops into our head is helping them solve their problem. After all, we don't want them to feel pain. But trying to fix someone's problem is a terrible idea. Most people want to feel heard and validated in their feelings. When you validate someone's feelings you are essentially saying, "Your feelings make sense to me." They don't want a fixer as a friend. If you shift your focus from fixing to validating feelings, you'll be a much wiser friend.

The next time you're with a friend, remember the word LEAD to help you listen attentively.

We must learn to listen to others with the heart of Christ. In other words, we are to listen incarnationally. Pete Scazzero puts it this way, "To listen incarnationally is to enter into another person's world, at a heart level, with the empathy of Christ, attending to their nonverbal clues as well as their words. This is how we demonstrate our love for them."[2]

Friendship Wisdom

Listen more than you talk.

Pause and Reflect

Think back over two recent conversations. Did you do more talking or listening? Sometimes you will be the one pouring out your heart, but often our focus needs to be on listening. Did you ask questions? What new insight did you learn about your friend from the conversation?

Pray

Holy One, I long to learn the art of incarnational listening. So often I find myself distracted by my own thousands of thoughts. Help me, Holy Spirit, to shift my focus and to offer my undivided attention to others. Teach me to look at them, to ask them more thoughtful questions to draw them out, and to listen with a heart to understand. I pray that You would free me from any tendency I have to try to fix others.

"A good friend knows when to be present,
when to listen, and how to always point me to God."

Edie Melson

Author, Director of Blue Ridge Mountain Writers Conference

CHAPTER 20

Avoid Gossip

A gossip betrays a confidence;
so avoid anyone who talks too much.

PROVERBS 20:19

Imagine being out with a friend who talks the entire time about mutual acquaintances. What happens in your soul? You feel uneasy. The first thought that comes to mind might be, "If she talks this way about *her*, what does she say about *me*?"

Gossip is not just reporting untrue facts. Often, it is painting another person in a poor light or sharing details that were meant to be confidential. The bottom line is that gossip erodes trust between friends. It makes others feel unsafe. This is why Solomon advised, "Avoid anyone who talks too much" (Prov. 20:19). That's great wisdom! Anyone who talks and talks and talks likely engages in gossip.

Google defines gossip as "casual or unconstrained conversation or reports about other people, typically involving details that are not confirmed as being true."[1] The word *unconstrained* gives the idea of a person who just talks and talks and doesn't stop. Often, that's when gossip happens. Proverbs warns us about gossip, but so do other parts of Scripture.

The apostle Paul wrote to the church in Corinth that he feared that there was "discord, jealousy, fits of rage, selfish ambition, slander, gossip, arrogance and disorder" in their church (2 Cor. 12:20b). That's quite the list, isn't it? Gossip is just as big a sin as the others. Yet often we seem to give ourselves a pass on this one.

The psalmist David also warns us. He writes that the person who may dwell in God's tent is the person "whose tongue utters no slander, who does no wrong to a neighbor, and casts no slur on others" (Ps. 15:3). I find that statement "casts no slur on others" interesting. We have the power to shape someone's view of another with our words. A good question to ask yourself is, whether spoken or written on social media, do my words cast another in an unfavorable light?

Three Action Steps to Help You Stop Gossip

Confess. If you find yourself starting to gossip, confess to the other person and ask forgiveness. Do it as soon as you find yourself going down that road. Just stop and then say something like, "I'm so sorry, I realize I was gossiping. Will you forgive me?"

Switch the conversation. If your friend starts to gossip, say something positive about the person being talked about. Offer grace. This is hard to do, but it's softer and easier than calling out your friend for gossiping. Try to set the example by speaking positively of others. However, if the pattern of gossip continues, then bring the issue gently out in the open and agree together to hold each other accountable.

Ask God to uproot your insecurity. When women engage in gossip, it usually comes from a place of insecurity. They join because they want others to like them or because they are trying to make themselves look better than whoever they are gossiping about. The problem is that gossip doesn't heal your insecurity. It adds to your wounds. Instead, next time you find yourself engaging in or listening to gossip, go to prayer and ask the Holy Healer to restore a sense of confidence in His love. You don't need to gossip to make friends. You don't need to gossip to build up your confidence.

Lying hidden under insecurity is often the attitude of judgmentalism. I realized this the other day in myself, as I was reflecting on a conversation I had with a friend. I had said something about another person that wasn't flattering. Looking back, I had done exactly what David warns against in Psalm 15. I had cast a slur on another's reputation. I had to spend significant time repenting and asking God to forgive me. Lying underneath the surface of my remark was the ugliness of judgmentalism. Jesus was very firm on the fact that we are not to stand in judgment of one another (Matt. 7:1).

I believe if we are going to enjoy the rich relationships that God intended for us to enjoy, we must be ruthless with gossip. The enemy will always tempt us in this way, but we have One who is greater. Jesus Himself is praying for you that you will be victorious!

Friendship Wisdom

Avoid gossip and gossipers.

Pause and Reflect

Consider when you are most likely to engage in gossip. With which of your friends do you feel the most comfortable doing this and why?

Pray

Oh, Lord, set a guard over my mouth! Teach me not to open the door to gossip of any kind. Honestly, Lord, this is hard. So often, someone shares something, and I enter in wanting the other person to feel understood and valued. But Lord, Your Word is clear that we are not to engage in gossip at all. So, help me. Bring conviction when the conversation starts moving in that direction. Free me to say something positive or to change the topic to steer away from gossip. When I fail, help me to confess fast and receive Your grace with open arms.

"A good friend is someone who listens well,
loves you through thick and thin,
points you to Jesus, prays for you,
prioritizes time with you,
and always has your back."

CRYSTAL PAINE
Author, Owner and Founder of Money Saving Mom, LLC

CHAPTER 21

Be Generous

The generous will themselves be blessed.

PROVERBS 22:9

Years ago, I was invited to Poland to do a conference for about a hundred Christian counselors. Alina brought me in an opened her home to extended uncommon generosity.[1] I traveled to Poland by myself, but Alina picked me up from the airport. She took me to a lovely lunch of crepes that are so popular in Poland. From there, she took me to her beautiful home. Alina, though she was a ministry leader and trained therapist, had her original degree in architecture. She told me how she had the privilege of designing their home and that it was a gift from God. She and her husband both felt because the Lord had been so generous to them that they should build an extra room in their house with a private bathroom. They called it the "Prophet's Room." Whenever a visiting speaker came, they offered the room for the speaker to rest, relax, and prepare. What a gift the prophet's room was to me personally on that trip. It was a space Alina and her husband had prayed over and dedicated to the Lord. Since that time, Alina has passed on to heaven and is now with the Lord.

Alina reminds me of the Shunammite woman who provided for Elisha. Whenever Elisha was in Shunem, this well-to-do woman offered him a meal. Then after a few times, she said to her husband, "I know this man who often comes our way is a holy man of God. Let's make a small room on the roof and put in it a bed and a table, a chair, and a lamp for him. Then he can stay there whenever he comes to us" (2 Kings 4:9–10). She realized God had blessed her, so she was happy to bless others. She provided for Elisha's needs generously with food and a place to stay.

Another biblical example of generosity is Tabitha, who is mentioned in the book of Acts. She is not described as wealthy but as one who was "always doing good and helping the poor" (Acts 9:36–42). She often used her sewing skills to make clothing for widows who might not have had enough money for basic necessities. Tabitha (also known as Dorcas) generously offered her talents.

My friend Bek is like Tabitha. Whenever I buy new jeans or pants, they are too long. I have often joked that I am going to have long legs when I get my new body in heaven. Thankfully, Bek is a generous friend. She hems all my pants, including my jeans. She's amazing!

Jesus instructed, "Freely you have received; freely give" (Matt. 10:8b). Pause for just a moment and consider, what have you been given as far as time, money, and talents? How can you give generously to your friends?

Researchers from the University of Wisconsin surveyed ten thousand 1957 Wisconsin high school graduates in their thirties about helping others at work; they were surveyed again thirty years later. What they discovered supports what Scripture teaches. Those who lived generous lives and helped others ended up being happier thirty years later in their sixties.[2] When we invest generously, we end up being refreshed.

What Does Generosity Look Like in Friendship?

Generous with your time. One of the biggest deterrents to rich friendship is busyness. If you don't have time to invest in friendships, you won't have any friends. We're all busy. But we can be generous with our time, even—and especially—when we're interrupted. Just this morning, I read that "the gospel of Mark records thirty-five times Jesus was interrupted. And each time, He made time for them."[3] When we offer our friends time in a generous way, we show that we love and value them.

Generous gift giving. Gifts can speak love. It's not that the gift has to be expensive; it's that it's thoughtful. I had randomly mentioned to my friend Gayle that I felt frustrated with organizing my earrings and some of my other jewelry. I couldn't figure out a good solution. The next day a package arrived for me from Amazon. When I opened it, there was a beautiful leather jewelry box from Gayle to help keep all my earrings organized. What a thoughtful gift! Gayle didn't have to do that. It was a gift reflective of her generous spirit. She knows me. Other times she has given me a Starbucks gift card because she knows I love coffee. I'm not the only one who has experienced Gayle's generosity. Many others have as well. Gayle takes seriously what Jesus said about living a generous life.

Generous notes and cards. In our digital age, we have forgotten the impact a written note can have on brightening someone's day. A simple note or card offering encouragement lifts the spirit. I have cards sitting on my desk as I write this, one from my friend Judy, one from Jill, one from Gayle, and a few others. They're little notes of appreciation. I'm sentimental, and those cards mean so much to me that I save them. When my soul feels dry, I can look back at them and receive refreshment from a friend's generous words. You have friends in your life who need a little encouragement. Why not pick up some note cards and handwrite them a note of encouragement? Buy a stamp and pop it in the mail. That tiny act will have a huge impact.

Generous prayers. One of the greatest ways we can demonstrate generosity in friendship is by praying often for our friends. Don't just offer a quick prayer. Instead, be generous with your prayer time. Spend time lifting your friends' concerns to the Father. Be willing to keep praying for the long haul. So often in prayer matters, we give up before we see an answer, assuming God isn't saying yes. However, the beauty of such prayers is that they continue. We show our generosity when we are willing to be persistent praying over the long haul.

Generosity is one of the most attractive qualities in a friend. If you want richer relationships, ask the Holy Spirit to replace your scarcity mindset with a generous attitude. Offer freely of your time, resources, and talents to invest in your friends. After all, those who are "generous will themselves be blessed" (Prov. 22:9).

Friendship Wisdom

Be generous today. Give an unexpected gift.

Pause and Reflect

What might prevent you from generously investing in your friends?

Pray

Lord, I am so grateful for Your generosity in my life. Thank You for Your lavish love toward me as demonstrated on the cross. Fill me with the same kind of love for others. Freely I have received so help me to freely give to others. Let Your love and generosity flow through me, I pray. Help me never to embrace a scarcity mindset.

CHAPTER 22

Monitor Your Expectations

Do not move an ancient boundary stone.

PROVERBS 23:10

Expectations can lead us into trouble, can't they?

Years ago, when my husband, Steve, was pastoring a small church, a woman came to the church and wanted to use her talent in the services. After a few weeks of attending, she volunteered to do sign language during worship and the preaching. Though we didn't have any hearing-impaired people attending, Steve rationalized that this might bring some new congregants, and what could go wrong? So, he enthusiastically invited the woman to begin signing the next Sunday. The only problem? The precious woman forgot to mention to Steve that she was a professional belly dancer. Let me just say, you've never seen such an "enthusiastic" signing!

Steve panicked. I remember him saying later, "Beck, what am I going to do?" Truthfully, I had no advice. After this went on for a couple of Sundays, Steve finally worked up the courage to tell her we no longer needed her services in the realm of signing. She left the church a few weeks later. We could have handled that with more grace and wisdom, but we were pretty young and lacked the experience to handle that type of delicate situation.

We all have expectations, but they can be a bit tricky. We conjure up an image of what will transpire in a situation or relationship, and when our expectations aren't met, we do one of two things. We either push harder to have them met or we retreat entirely. I've witnessed both responses among friends. However, the most common response I've seen is when one friend feels pressured by another and backs up. What does all this have to do with ancient boundary stones like Solomon talked about in Proverbs 23:10? I'm glad you asked.

In ancient times, boundary stones marked property lines. When Solomon wrote that we are not to move ancient boundary stones, he was referring to respecting the property lines of others. We are not to take advantage of others. One way we take advantage of others is to not respect their personal boundaries. Earlier in the book, we talked about getting better at setting our own boundaries. However, in this chapter, we're talking about monitoring our expectations to respect the boundaries of others.

Relationships are built on mutual respect. Each of us has God-given limits. Those limits must be honored if we are going to thrive. When we push too hard on another's boundaries, relationships dissolve. I have too often seen unrealistic expectations ruin the beauty of friendship. Let me give you just a few examples:

Within the context of marriage, either spouse might have extraordinary expectations. When their expectations are not met, the friendship within the marriage goes belly up. If you're going to cultivate a deep friendship with your spouse, you cannot expect them to be everything to you!

Within friendships between women, at times one friend places undue pressure on the other to spend more time together than is reasonable. Or to text back the moment their message is received. That just stirs up anxiety and unrest. No one wants that pressure. Or, perhaps, one gets jealous that her friend is spending more time with other friends. She stews, "She's my bestie!" As a result, she places undue pressure on her supposed "bestie." Another area where expectations become a problem is in finding agreement. Maybe one friend mistakenly believes that to be a close friend, you must agree on everything. Realistically, that's not possible. Each of us holds our own opinions and convictions. Your closest friends might agree with you on your big values, like your belief in Jesus or your view of Scripture. But they may not agree with you politically or about different social issues.

We must be careful not to place undue pressure on our friends, expecting them to be more than they can be to us. But you might be wondering, how do I monitor my expectations so that they don't become unrealistic? Here are a few ways.

Practical Ideas for Monitoring Expectations

Cultivate gratitude in your friendship with Christ. The more you cultivate thankfulness in your friendship with Christ, the less you will tend to grow frustrated with others. Gratitude replaces entitlement. So, when you find yourself disappointed, grab a journal and start a "thankful" list. You'll be amazed at how your attitude will change.

Surrender and release your desires. The entirety of our spiritual journeys with Jesus is a trek of surrender. We release what we can't hold on to in order to gain what we cannot lose. As we continually let go of our expectations, the Lord is faithful to strengthen our trust in Him.

Do something kind when you feel disappointed. At some point or another, every friend will let us down in some way. In the moments when you feel disappointed, remember the times when you have also disappointed others. Then, take action, and do something kind for someone else. Mail a card, treat your friend to a cup of coffee, send flowers. The point is to keep kindness flowing out of your heart. The more kindness flows, the less likely bitterness and resentment grow.

When you respect the limits of others, your friendships become life-giving and flourishing. Offering the gift of freedom in friendship is a beautiful gift. Ask the Holy Spirit to empower you to give this gift to others.

Friendship Wisdom

Learn to surrender your expectations, offering your friends freedom instead.

Pause and Reflect

When have you placed unrealistic expectations on others? How did you handle your disappointment when your expectations weren't met?

Pray

Lord God, I confess that at times my expectations of friends have put undue pressure on them. Show me, I pray, how to release and surrender my expectations, trusting You to satisfy my deepest longings. Thank You, Lord Jesus, that You are the friend who never fails. You are the friend who satisfies my soul. Help me to fix my focus on You today and to let go of any hurt I have experienced in the friendship department.

CHAPTER 23

Choose Your Closest Friends Wisely

Do not make friends with a hot-tempered person,
do not associate with one easily angered.

PROVERBS 22:24

Recently, my husband, Steve, gave a rather profound message on the types of friends he wants in his close circle. As I reflected on his message, I remembered times in my life when I have been unwise in who I became friends with. Once I became friends quickly with someone only to discover how prone to gossip she was. Another soon exhibited a pattern of negativity and criticalness. Still another time, I befriended someone who grew easily annoyed, which left me feeling as if I were walking on eggshells.

Scripture teaches that while we are to love everyone, we are only to become close friends with certain people. I've thought long and hard about the type of friends I want. I want close friends who understand my heart for prayer. I want close friends who are positive and don't continually see the worst in every situation. I want friends who will offer me grace and yet inspire me to walk even closer with Jesus. And I want friends who aren't easily offended.

Solomon encouraged us to choose our friends wisely. Rightly so. The more time you spend with people, the more inclined you are to become like them: "Don't make friends with a hot-tempered person, do not associate with one easily angered" (Prov. 22:24). Solomon also wrote that we are to avoid those who are given to gossip (Prov. 20:19) and that we are to walk with the wise if we want to become wise (Prov. 13:20). In other words, we are to choose our closest friends carefully.

When I think of the type of friends I want in my closest inner circle, the words of Paul come to mind: "I want to know Christ—yes, to know the power of his resurrection and the participation of his sufferings, becoming like him in his death" (Phil. 3:10). Lest I sound morbid, let me explain. It's not that I'm longing to suffer, but I know suffering is a part of this life. Rather, my overall aim in life is to know Christ better. Therefore, I want close friends who are on that same journey, longing to know Christ better, to become like Him in His death. As these friends press into Jesus, I am encouraged to press in more deeply too. I'm guessing those are the kind of friends you long for as well.

Three Questions to Ask Before Moving Forward in a Friendship

Who in my circle of friends is pursuing Jesus intentionally? Friends who fix their focus on Christ are a treasure. Watch for friends who make Jesus the center of their lives. Those are amazing companions to have on your journey. Now, to clarify, this doesn't mean you never become friends with those who don't share your faith. Those are friends with whom you can model the love of Christ. However, the friends who are passionate to know Jesus more intimately will be the dearest.

Who do I see exemplifying integrity? I don't want to have to wonder about someone's integrity. Likely, you don't either. The dearest friends are those who are honest, vulnerable, and truthful. Friends of integrity won't talk behind your back or use you for their own personal gain. Instead, they'll take your hand and say, "Let's journey closer to Jesus together." Their yes is yes, and their no is no. You won't need to worry about duplicity with these friends.

Who feels safe and offers grace? Trying to be friends with someone who is easily angered is like trying to walk on eggshells without breaking them. You end up feeling nervous every time you're around them. On the other hand, friends who offer grace and understanding are safe. They're not looking for something to criticize. They are too busy monitoring their walk of holiness to be judging others. The last thing you need in your life is someone monitoring your every move, waiting to pounce with criticism. Friends who offer grace are the safest.

Close friends are a treasure, but to build the bond that lasts decades, learn to invest your time in friends who demonstrate these qualities: They pursue Jesus, exemplify integrity, and offer grace.

Friendship Wisdom

Pray for discernment when trying to decide who to move closer to in friendship.

Pause and Reflect

Consider the history you've had with some of your friends. Which are the friendships that you desire to pursue for the long haul? Have there been any friendships that you thought would be long-term term only to feel disappointed along the way? What changed in those friendships?

Pray

Lord, though I love all my friends, I pray that You would increase my discernment for who should be in my innermost circle. Help me to walk closely with those who pursue You passionately. Thank You that You are present with me always and that when I call, You promise to answer. Fill me, I pray, with renewed wisdom and discernment in all my friendships that I might choose wisely the friends I pull closest.

"A good friend is wise and discerning,
first in the things of God,
and second in their heart.
They offer themselves without any expectation of returned love."

Blythe Daniel

Author, Literary Agent

CHAPTER 24

Don't Give Envy a Seat at Your Table

Do not let your heart envy.
PROVERBS 23:17

Envy wreaks havoc in friendships. I've seen the damage to many relationships because jealousy is like throwing a grenade into a relationship. It leaves others wounded and damaged.

Here are just a few scenarios . . .

Celine becomes jealous when she realizes that her coworker, Krista, has now become close with someone else. In her jealous state, Celine starts tracking Krista's every move and watching every post on social media to see if Krista is spending more time with her new friend.

Marie sees a post with a photo of some of her friends meeting for coffee. She wonders why she wasn't invited and then starts spinning stories in her mind about how her friends don't care about her.

Solomon wrote, "Do not let your heart envy" (Prov. 23:17). You and I have fabulous minds. We can direct our thoughts to where we want them to focus, which means when we start to feel envious, we can catch those thoughts and not allow them to take up space in our brains. On the other hand, if we dwell on those thoughts, it will be to our demise and the demise of our friendships. This is what happened to Saul in the Old Testament.

After David slayed the giant, Goliath, the women began chanting, "Saul has slain his thousands, and David his tens of thousands" (1 Sam. 18:7). That was all Saul needed to hear. He became insanely jealous, and his view of David changed. Saul's jealousy became so intense that he hurled a spear at David to kill him. Thankfully, David dodged the spear. God kept giving David success and victory in whatever he put his hand to and this drove Saul nuts.

Our jealousy can easily morph into obsession. Instead of being grateful for what God has done in our lives, we become haunted by the success or victories He is giving others. When we become consumed with what another has that we don't have, not only does it leave us discontented, but our jealousy also leaves us vulnerable to unhealthy thinking.

How Do We Keep Jealousy Out of Our Friendships?

Take every thought captive (2 Cor. 10:5). The minute you feel yourself sliding toward jealousy, take that thought captive. Confess your sin to the Lord and surrender your thought life to the Holy Spirit. Don't allow jealousy to grow. Don't rationalize it or nurture it. It is exceedingly dangerous, not only for your friendships but also for your mental and emotional health. Switch your focus to the Lord and the wonder of His character. Praise Him for His grace and goodness in your life.

Cultivate contentment by choosing gratitude. As human beings, it seems we always want more. Our focus is drawn to what we're lacking rather than to the beautiful gifts we have received. When you find yourself feeling jealous, take a few moments and make a list of every blessing in your life. Then spend time intentionally worshiping and praising Him.

Jesus is enough! He is the only one who can completely satisfy. Until we find our contentment in Him, we will always crave more.

Let go of trying to control your friend. We can never control another person. We can't control who they choose to become close with or who they choose to hang out with. We also can't control the amount of success God gives them. When jealousy becomes toxic, often control enters the picture. One person tries to control the other. I have seen this in some relationships. I remember years ago when one of my friends became jealous that another friend was spending more time with me. The one stepped in and tried to manipulate and control the other in an effort to keep her close. It actually backfired, because the friend felt smothered. The best thing to do is to ask God to help you let go and give your friends freedom.

Jealousy has the potential to be one of the deadliest sins if you give it room to grow. It can become toxic and ultimately damages healthy relationships. Be ruthless with surrendering it to the Lord. As you surrender and ask God to fill you with contentment, you will enjoy much deeper friendships and much stronger mental health.

Friendship Wisdom

Cultivate contentment in your friendships.

Pause and Reflect

Have there been seasons of jealousy in your life where your envy has impacted your friendships? How did that impact you personally?

Pray

Lord Jesus, I realized how deadly jealousy is for my relationships. I pray for the grace to take this sin seriously and to uproot any envious thought before it grows. Create in me a clean heart, I pray. As I cultivate a contented spirit, would You settle any insecurity lurking within? Instead, fill me with holy confidence that assures me that You are on time in my life.

CHAPTER 25

Bring These Three Treasures to Your Friendships

By wisdom a house is built,
and through understanding, it is established;
through knowledge its rooms are filled
with rare and beautiful treasures.

PROVERBS 24:3–4

Several years ago, my husband, Steve, told me about buried treasure in the Rocky Mountains. Apparently, a millionaire named Forrest Fenn buried treasure in the mountains and challenged people to go hiking to find it. Honestly, the tale seemed far-fetched. I told Steve I was going to fact-check him. Well, guess what? It turns out the story is not just a legend but a true story. Forrest Fenn, who was diagnosed with cancer, wrote a memoir called *The Thrill of the Chase*. That title alone would draw in my husband, who loves a great adventure! In his book, Fenn wrote a poem that supposedly contained clues for where to find the treasure of gold and other valuables. The hunt began in 2010 when thousands started hunting and hiking to find the treasure. A thirty-two-year-old Michigan native and medical student Jack Stuef was the person who finally solved Fenn's poem.[1]

Treasure chests are intriguing, aren't they? At a local restaurant, my little granddaughters love to choose a treasure from the huge treasure chest in the lobby after they eat. The chest is filled with beaded necklaces, stickers, and other trinkets.

If you were to bring your friend a chest of treasures, what would you put inside? Jewelry, books, coffee cups, nail polish, bath salts? What if you were to consider giving your friends other treasures? There are treasures that can't be bought, but they are invaluable in solidifying deep connections. They are mentioned in Proverbs 24:34; we could paraphrase the verse like this: By wisdom a friendship is built, and through understanding it is established; through knowledge its rooms are filled with rare and beautiful treasures.

Let's unpack that a bit more.

Three Treasures to Give Your Friends

Wisdom. When we bring wisdom to our friendships, they thrive. Wisdom shows up in how we respect boundaries, how we pray for and cheer on our friends, and how we listen. Wise friends bring immeasurable blessings to my life. They thoughtfully consider what I share with them, they encourage and cheer me on in the pursuits that God has called me to, and they are faithful to pray. They aren't judgmental. They wisely consider all sides of issues and invite me into the process. That's also the type of friend I endeavor to be.

Understanding. Solomon writes that "through understanding it is established." The idea here is of resetting what's been toppled. I love that. It reminds me of when our kids were growing up and all playing sports. I can't count the number of times lamps were knocked over by a flying soccer ball. Our kids would then stop the ball and reestablish the lamp.

Life has a way of knocking us over. A good friend will step in and help us reestablish a firm footing. They do this by offering empathy. They show you through their actions that your feelings make sense to them. Maybe they do this by taking you to a doctor's appointment and sitting through treatments. Or by allowing you to process all your mixed-up feelings.

I remember my friend Gail, who has since gone home to be with the Lord. When I returned home from several days in the hospital after undergoing a six-hour double mastectomy, there were brand-new soft sheets on the bed in our master bedroom. Gail knew I would need a tiny bit of encouragement. She understood how vulnerable I would feel after the surgery, and she stepped in to help reestablish me.

Knowledge. Before you jump to any conclusions about showing up as a friend with knowledge, that's not what this means. It means taking time to get to know someone and bringing your knowledge of that person into the friendship. Let me give you an example. My friend Keri knows that my favorite color is blue. My phone has a blue case, and I use blue for as many book covers as I'm allowed. I just love blue! Last year, when I needed to order a new computer, I felt overwhelmed. Technology is not my thing, and I wasn't sure which computer to buy. Keri, who is way more techy than I am, stepped in and took over ordering for me. Imagine my delight when I picked up my new Mac and it was blue! What a thoughtful gesture. I felt so known. May I ask you? How well do you know your friends? What are their favorite colors, flowers, books, passages of Scripture, coffee drinks, and clothing styles? It is a treasure to have a friend who puts the effort into knowing all about you.

When you offer these three treasures to your friends, you are going to find that the relationship grows much richer, and as a result, you're going to feel more deeply connected.

Friendship Wisdom

Bring the treasures of wisdom, understanding, and knowledge into your friendships.

Pause and Reflect

Think about a good friend. Consider some questions you might ask your friend to gain more knowledge about them and to offer more understanding.

Pray

> *God, I praise You and thank You that You treasure me. Your Word teaches me that I am precious and honored in Your sight (Isa. 43:4). Help me, Lord, to follow Your example and to view my friendships as precious. Show me how to bring the treasures of wisdom, understanding, and knowledge into my friendships so that each of my friends feels valued and known.*

CHAPTER 26

Choose Vulnerability

Do not exalt yourself.
PROVERBS 25:6

Cancer was very clarifying for me. When I was walking through the dark valley of breast cancer, I learned about vulnerability in a whole new way. I remember I had scheduled my oldest daughter's graduation party. A hundred invitations had gone out. Yet I was now scheduled for a double radical mastectomy about a week before the party. I remember wondering, How on earth am I going to cancel the party? My daughter will feel so disappointed. I had no idea what to do! But my friend Kathy stepped in without my even asking. When she realized the timing of the surgery and the timing of the party, she told me she would take over the party. She orchestrated a few other friends to help, and they came in like the graduation party brigade! The party went beautifully! I still feel foggy just thinking about how she ran the whole event. I ended up going back to bed because I was so exhausted, but our daughter felt celebrated and loved.

Vulnerability means that when you feel weak, you allow others to step in to help, empathize, and comfort.

My friend Ashley learned about vulnerability through her journey with miscarriage.[1] After several miscarriages, she battled deep, dark discouragement. She discovered that holding the pain on her own was not working, so she reached out to several trusted friends to share the depth of her grief. By reaching out and making herself vulnerable, Ashley found that her friendships grew deeper, and she no longer felt quite as isolated. Her friends came alongside her as she grieved. They prayed for her and supported her by bringing meals, checking in, and offering empathy.

Often, instead of choosing vulnerability, we edit what version of ourselves others will see. We strive to be independent, yet nowhere in Scripture is independence affirmed. We strive to present a better image. But the prophet Isaiah wrote, "The images that are carried about are burdensome, a burden for the weary" (Isa. 46:1b). Trying to be independent or keep up an image is exhausting. How much more refreshing is it to simply choose vulnerability?

Vulnerability involves risk and trust. To let others see your weaknesses, there has to be trust in the strength of the relationship. Vulnerability isn't weakness. Quite the opposite; it takes courage to reveal your faults and fragile places. Vulnerability involves emotional exposure.

This is why it's important to use discretion. As author Alli Worthington posted on her Instagram account, "Not everyone deserves a front-row seat in your life. Choose wisely."[2] On the other hand, if you never dare to be vulnerable with friends, your friendship will get stuck and not go as deep as it might.

Why Is Vulnerability So Important in Friendship?

We can only offer and receive comfort by choosing vulnerability. Paul wrote in 2 Corinthians 1, "Praise be to the God and Father of our Lord Jesus Christ, the Father of compassion and the God of all comfort, who comforts us in all our troubles, so that we can comfort those in any trouble, with the comfort we receive from God" (vv. 3–4). We are to comfort each other in our relationships just as we have received comfort from God Himself. Paul goes on to write later in this chapter that he wanted his friends in Corinth to be aware that when he was in Asia, he had experienced great pressure, far beyond his ability to endure, to the point that he almost despaired of life itself (2 Cor. 1:8). Notice, Paul made himself vulnerable by sharing that he experienced great pressure and despair. It's remarkable to me that he trusted his friends in Corinth with that information. If you read through the letters he wrote to the Corinthian church, that church was a mess! I think his show of trust is profound. Even though these Christians were broken, Paul trusted them enough to make himself vulnerable. He needed their prayers and support.

We can only support each other in prayer as we are vulnerable. Prayer is the way we carry each other's burdens before the Father. Here's an example. Recently, I found myself fighting vague discouragement. Instead of waking with my usual joy, I woke with anxiety and a heavy heart. I couldn't figure out what was wrong. Overall, life was going well, but there were aspects I simply felt discouraged about. After a few days of this, I confided to a close friend about how I was feeling and asked for prayer. That friend began to fight for me on her knees and checked in with me over the next few weeks to see if I was feeling better. About a week after she started praying, the heaviness lifted. My circumstances did not change, but my joy returned. Looking back, what if I had not made myself vulnerable to ask for prayer? Often, I find that people are reluctant to share prayer requests with others, valuing privacy over vulnerability. The problem with that is that we are told in Scripture to carry one another's burdens (Gal. 6:2). How can we comfort and carry if we don't know what those burdens are?

We can only enjoy the gift of empathy when we make ourselves vulnerable. Vulnerability opens the door for us to receive empathy. All of us need empathy—knowing that our feelings make sense to someone. When we receive empathy, we feel a deep connection. Similarly, as mentioned before, when we offer empathy, we also feel that deep connection. This is why reciprocity within the realm of vulnerability is so important.

Jesus invites us to the path of vulnerability that He chose. He made Himself vulnerable by becoming man and by becoming obedient even to death (Phil. 2:8). He didn't cling to His rights as God's Son. Vulnerability is essential for us as well, especially if we are going to enjoy the rich relationships God desires for us. Choose wisely. You don't have to share intimate details with everyone. However, a few close friends with whom you make yourself vulnerable become stretcher bearers for you. They lift you before the Father and encourage you in your journey. They become a life-giving community around you.

Friendship Wisdom

Vulnerability is a key ingredient to close friendships.

Pause and Reflect

Who are three friends with whom you can be vulnerable? Are they also vulnerable with you? How has this strengthened your friendship?

Pray

Lord Jesus, You made Yourself vulnerable for me. Scripture teaches me that You humbled Yourself, taking the place of a servant. In the garden of Gethsemane, You told Your friends that You needed them to stay awake with You. Your heart was in the deepest place of grief and sorrow, and You needed them to keep watch and pray. You made Yourself so vulnerable that You even went to the cross for me. Lord, help me to follow Your example. Help me not to cling to my image at the expense of sharing authentically with others. Holy One, fill me with wisdom as I embark on this journey of vulnerability. Show me who I can trust to support me when I feel fragile.

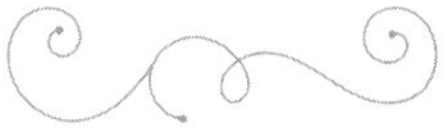

"A good friend is someone who holds your heart gently,
knows your imperfections
and loves you through the seasons of life."

Debbie Alsdorf

Literary Agent, Author, Speaker

CHAPTER 27

Let Go of Defensiveness

Enemies disguise themselves with their lips.
PROVERBS 26:24

I felt attacked and accused. My mind started spinning, and I sputtered out incoherent phrases, like "I'm not!" "I didn't." I was definitely triggered. I was taken back to moments when, as a little girl, my mom, who struggled with mental illness, would attack me verbally. She could be loving one moment, and then a switch would flip, and she would become emotionally abusive. When she got enraged, I became defenseless. There was no making sense of it, and no way to win. I shrank on the outside, but inwardly, anger broiled.

Later, as an adult, I was attending a small function and an acquaintance asked to speak with me privately. I said "sure," but inside, fear began growing. I knew she was upset. I was tired. I was in the middle of a huge transition and not functioning on all cylinders. We went to a private space, and then she began lobbing criticisms at me and accusing me of all sorts of wrong motives. I was taken back to childhood to those moments when I felt like the Rolodex of my mind spun and everything I knew to be true would fly out of my head. As a result, I would grow paralyzed and not know how to respond. In this case, rather than handling the situation like an emotionally healthy adult, I tried to make myself look innocent. Instead of drawing out the other person using phrases like "tell me more," I went into defensive reactive mode. My husband heard what was transpiring and came to rescue me.

Looking back, I realize how dangerous triggers are when we're criticized or even lovingly confronted. It becomes easy to become defensive. As a result, acquaintances become enemies and friendships shatter. In the situation I described above, I should have remained calm. I didn't. I should have invited my acquaintance to tell me more. I didn't. I should have apologized for giving her the impression that I didn't care. I didn't do that. Instead, I reacted.

As we mature in Christ, we are called to become more like Christ in our relationships. Jesus, when falsely accused, did not lash out in a reactive spirit. Instead, He responded with questions (John 18:28–37). He didn't disguise Himself or grow defensive. He remained calm and responded with wisdom. Oh, to be like Jesus! I don't know about you, but I still have a long way to go in terms of godly transformation. It's so easy when we are criticized to feel triggered and powerless to react and become defensive.

Defensiveness often shows up in blame-shifting. Whether consciously or subconsciously, we blame others for our bad behavior. An example of this is in the Old Testament book of Exodus, when Moses was gone a long time communing with God. The people grew impatient and asked Aaron to make them a new god. Aaron had them take off all their gold jewelry, and he fashioned it into a golden calf. When Moses came down from the mountain, he was furious and confronted Aaron. However, Aaron became defensive and said essentially, "Hey, don't blame me! The people grew impatient and asked me to make them an idol. I had them take off their gold. I threw it into the fire and out popped this calf!" (Ex. 32:21–24). Talk about defensiveness and blame-shifting! Aaron's excuse is almost laughable, yet the truth is, sometimes we're just like Aaron. Someone confronts us, we don't want to look bad, so we defend ourselves by blaming others.

How Do We Let Go of Defensiveness and Blame-Shifting?

Examine your triggers. If we're going to let go of defensiveness in our friendships first, I believe we need to do a deep dive into what triggers us in conflict. Triggers are an emotional reaction based on past experiences. Sometimes those past experiences were traumatic. As a result, we may react in a way that is disproportionate to the current situation. When trying to figure out what those triggers are, it can be helpful to ask yourself a few questions. Keep in mind: Triggers can make us react in an emotionally immature way. Rather than responding with wisdom, we grow defensive.

Here are some questions I recommend asking yourself to help you figure out your triggers:

1. How was conflict handled in your family of origin?
2. When you were disciplined as a child, what did that look like?
3. Did you experience any trauma in your growing-up years? How might that trauma affect the way you respond in adulthood?
4. In your adulthood, where have you experienced deep hurt? For example, many have experienced church hurt. As a result, when they encounter anything difficult in their church experience, they run, rage, or become cynical because they don't want to be hurt again.

Accept responsibility. Beyond examining your triggers, practice accepting responsibility for whatever you can when criticized. This doesn't mean you apologize for things you didn't do, but it does mean if there's an element of any truth in the criticism, you take ownership.

If you want your friendships to deepen, don't hide behind defensiveness. Learn to examine your triggers and accept responsibility where you can. As a result, your relationships will not be bound to pretense, they'll be rooted in authenticity.

Friendship Wisdom

Don't become defensive when criticized. Instead, pause. Be aware of your triggers and take ownership where you are accountable.

Pause and Reflect

Think back on the last time you were criticized. Did you grow defensive? Did you blame shift? Did you take ownership for anything?

Pray

> *Oh, Lord Jesus, I admit and confess that at times when I'm criticized, my natural instinct is to become defensive. As I read through the gospels and how You interacted with those who criticized You, I realize You never disguised Yourself or attempted to make Yourself look better. I long to be more like You Lord Jesus, but I realize how desperately I need You to change my heart. Holy Spirit, I pray that You would fill me and help me to stand confidently in who You say I am and not to hide behind defensiveness in any of my relationships.*

CHAPTER 28

Love Well Today, You Might Not Have Tomorrow

Do not boast about tomorrow,
for you do not know what a day may bring.
PROVERBS 27:1

Bev met Gary on a blind date. They moved from friendship to love, got married, and raised their kids together. Gary was a pastor, and Bev directed women's ministries at their church.

Through the years, their love for each other grew. They shared the common interest of a calling to ministry, having fun together, raising their family together, and working well together. Then the unthinkable happened. Gary was diagnosed with a rare form of eye cancer. As Gary's cancer progressed, it became obvious that the cancer would be fatal.

Near the end of Gary's life, Bev wrote me these words—"We are just trying to spoil each other and love each other well every day, because we don't know how many days we have left." I never forgot her words, though it's been several years. What great wisdom for life and friendship!

Just the other day, I had a lovely and rich visit with a friend. She had unexpectedly flown into town and was able to spend the day with me. We had lunch, went for coffee, did a little shopping, laughed, and prayed together. We talked about our grandkids, our marriages, and our ministries. Throughout the day, I remember thinking, "These moments are precious! I want to be fully present and treasure each one." I want to love well because I don't know what tomorrow holds.

Yet what's true for all of us is that in the busyness of life, with its deadlines and demands, it's easy to take our friendships for granted. We mistakenly presume that our friends will always be there. But the clock is ticking, and time is passing.

None of us knows how many more days we have with loved ones. None of us knows how many hours we have left with our friends. In light of that uncertainty, we need to love well today because we can't boast that we have tomorrow.

James, the brother of Jesus, warned us that we cannot make this boast because life is but a mist that's here for a little while and then vanishes (James 4:14–15). That's sobering, isn't it? James then goes on to teach us that if we know the right thing to do but we don't do it, it's sin (James 4:17).

How do we boast about tomorrow in our relationships? One way is by putting off the good that God asks us to do. We rationalize, "I can do that tomorrow." Maybe we think, "I can repair that friendship later when I'm less stressed." Or, "I can get to know my neighbors when my life settles down a bit." Or, "I can apologize to my spouse tomorrow for being harsh." But what if tomorrow never comes? We end up leaving undone what God intended us to do, and the bottom line is: That is sin. How much better for our relationships, to keep short accounts? How much wiser is it to take immediate action to repair when we've fractured a friendship?

Don't put off what you can do today to make someone feel valued. My friend Karen lives this way.

Karen has recently retired. She has lots of friends and activities she's involved with, tennis, Bible study, and traveling with her retired husband. But recently she said to my husband, who was visiting, "I get to spend the whole day with my mother!" Karen knows she doesn't have much longer with her aging mom. Though her life is very full, she ensures that her mama feels seen, heard, cherished.

If you want to be friend-wise, prioritize that friendship today!

Friendship Wisdom

Don't put off being the friend God is calling you to be to someone today. Only God knows what tomorrow holds. Live your life as if it's your last day.

Pause and Reflect

How prone are you to put off hanging out with friends because of busyness or work? How has that played out for your friendships in the past?

Pray

Holy One, thank You that You pursue me continually. I praise You that today, I have the opportunity to show my friends how much I love them. Help me not to procrastinate in showing love or making things right because I don't know if I have tomorrow. Teach me to live with the awareness that today is the day to value and love people as You do.

CHAPTER 29

Run After Relationships Rather Than Riches

The rich are wise in their own eyes; one who is poor and discerning sees how deluded they are.

Proverbs 28:11

I read some interesting statistics about how long it takes to establish friendships. In a Kansas University News report, author Rick Helman quoted research conducted by a colleague who discovered that it takes about fifty hours of time together to move from being acquaintances to being casual friends; it takes ninety hours to go from that stage to a more solid friendship, and get this, it takes more than two hundred hours of being together before you consider someone a close friend![1] Isn't that fascinating?

That research may leave you with the thought, "Who has time for friendships?"

In our over-scheduled lives, we're running, but the question is, what are we running after? We often condone a busy life as a valuable life, but as a result, relationships and friendships have often taken a back seat. However, this has led to a staggering epidemic of loneliness. Busyness is one of the leading factors in feeling isolated because you can't have life-giving friendships unless you slow down long enough to invest in them. Busyness might just be the bane of our existence.

If you want close friends, you must slow down!

There was a season in my life when I was crazy busy. I started to notice that people were saying to me, "I know how busy you are, but I'd love to get together." The COVID pandemic hit, and everything shut down. The pandemic provided a wonderful opportunity to reexamine my life. I had the time to sit before the Lord and consider my heart's deepest desires. I realized, in my hours with Him, that busyness and productivity were no longer satisfying me. I missed spending time with my close friends. Now, if you know me, you might be wondering, "Becky, *did* you slow down?" Yes. I am still writing, speaking, and podcasting. However, the rhythm of all that is a bit slower. I have created more space in my life to have lunch with friends or enjoy long phone calls with close friends. I've become more tuned to staying present in every relationship, and whether I am reading a story to a grandchild or having coffee with a friend, I am seeking to be fully there in my thinking rather than letting my mind wander to what is happening next.

Solomon wrote that a person who runs after riches is deluded. It's not that it's wrong to be wealthy. God blesses some people with extraordinary wealth so that they in turn can bless others. What Solomon is saying is that it is foolish to spend your time chasing wealth. I think we can also apply this principle to chasing status, a bigger platform, or increased power. The warning is clear. Stop running after things that will fade. Instead, consider how you are spending your time.

God wants you deeply connected with Him, which takes time, and deeply invested in life-giving friendships, which also takes time. The question is, what are you doing with your time? Where does the bulk of it go?

I know that some are more extroverted and some are more introverted, but all of us were created for deep connection and belonging. Those types of relationships take time. If we don't put any of our effort into that, we are not going to live the abundant life Jesus invited us to live. While extroverts might enjoy a greater quantity of friends, introverts still need deep friendships. Introverts might need more space for quiet and time alone, but none of us is to live an isolated life. We need to feel connected, and that is going to take time. Deep connections don't just happen in a hot second. They take time.

In light of that, I'd like to suggest that you track how you're using your time over the next week. Write down where every hour goes. Then analyze the results, asking yourself first, "Am I investing in my relationship with God? How much time do I give that?" Ask yourself, "How much time did I spend this week investing in relationships with friends?" If you didn't spend a lot of time in either place, figure out where your time went. Did it all go to earning money? Did it go to Netflix, or social media, or striving to reach another level of status? Only you can answer those questions. But I think they are worth considering.

Moses wrote, "Teach us to number our days, that we may gain a heart of wisdom" (Ps. 90:12). Wise living includes well-connected friendships, which may mean we need to say no to other things, so that we have the time to invest in our friends.

Friendship Wisdom

Slow down so that you can have the hours to invest in your friendships.

Pause and Reflect

What takes up the most time in your day? How does that time commitment match the friendships you value?

Prayer

Lord Jesus, I realize that so often I get sucked into hurry and busyness even though that's not in alignment with my values. Realign my heart with Yours, I pray. Help me to prioritize people over projects. I pray that I will create the space to be fully present with friends. I realize that if I am going to enjoy the friendships my heart desires that I must slow down enough to enjoy conversation. Help me not to anesthetize my loneliness with scrolling on my phone or zoning out on media. Instead, help me to put the time and effort into pursuing genuine friendships.

CHAPTER 30

Put on Strength and Dignity

She is clothed with strength and dignity;
she can laugh at the days to come.
PROVERBS 31:25

I think many of us feel we would be able to walk with strength and dignity if life just went a little better. However, I think strength and dignity might be best forged in the fire of adversity. Certainly, that's been true in my friend Gayle's life.

When Gayle gave birth to her daughter, they knew instantly something was wrong. Missy was diagnosed with spina bifida and transferred immediately to a different hospital 390 miles away. Missy had to go through surgery to close up the hole on her spine and had to have a shunt put in her head due to hydrocephalus. After the surgeries, the doctors discovered a severe breathing problem, and once again, Missy's hospital stay was extended. After being apart from her infant for three weeks, Gayle and her husband traveled with their toddler son to the hospital where Missy was. Again, Gayle and her husband were told their infant could not come home. They had to transfer her to a full-time nursing facility. The time in the care unit was extended another three to four months. When Gayle was informed once again that she could not bring her infant home, her heart was broken! Gayle went by herself into the nursery and placed her hands on Missy's empty crib and cried out to God as never before. She begged Him to fill that empty crib. Two days later, the doctors called and told Gayle to come pick up her baby.

Through her daughter's life, Gayle has had to develop a resilience that is only rooted in her faith in God. Missy has had countless surgeries, and yet today, she has grown into a remarkable woman.

After I asked Gayle to recount her story for me, she told me that she was so grateful to look back and remember how faithful God had been through the years. As a result, Gayle worshiped Him for continuously sustaining them.

Gayle is a woman of strength and dignity who has learned those character traits through the long, hard journey of raising a child with a severe disability. She never lost her sense of humor, and rather than growing bitter, Gayle grew stronger. Today, her life and words bless many of her friends, including me. She is friend-wise in every way. I see the fruit of Gayle trusting God through those dark days. She possesses strength (an inner quiet confidence) and dignity (worthy of honor and respect) combined with a sense of humor that is contagious!

Here's what I know—women of strength and dignity make better friends. They're not easily offended and don't get snippy when things don't go their way. They have learned what's important and what's not. They laugh easily and bless their friends.

How to Become a Woman of Strength and Dignity

Cultivate deep trust in God even when life is hard. Now, let me be clear; trusting God doesn't mean you're not going to grieve. Life is hard. It is going to throw unexpected curveballs at you. Grieving is holy. Be authentic in your sorrow. But learn to cling to what you know to be true about God, even when you don't understand. Cultivate a long journey of trust in God so that when the hard times come, your faith holds strong.

Keep your sense of humor. Solomon wrote that the woman of strength and dignity can laugh at the days to come (Prov. 31:25). Even in the moments when life feels challenging ask God to show you funny little moments in the journey. It's not that you will diminish the pain; it's that laughter is good for our souls. Seek to navigate life with a sense of humor.

Speak wise words of blessing. This takes practice, but it is so worth the effort. You can begin by praying blessings for your friends. After writing a blog post on "3 Prayers of Blessing to Pray for Your Friends,"[1] I received emails from readers who thought it was a wonderful idea. Your friends need and want to be blessed. As you start with prayer, an attitude of blessing and cheering for your friends will naturally flow from your life. And who doesn't want to be friends with someone who blesses and cheers them on? Women of dignity speak with wisdom, and they bless others. The world has enough sharp critics and cynical naysayers. Use your words to bring hope and healing to others.

Strength and dignity don't come easily. It's not a matter of having a calm personality. You become a woman of honor as you make wise choices along the way, even when life is tremendously hard. Despite all Gayle has gone through in her journey as Missy's mom, she has chosen to lean into God rather than pull away from Him.

Friendship Wisdom

Seek to become a woman of strength and dignity by nurturing deep trust in God, keeping your sense of humor, and speaking wise words of blessing. As a result, you won't lack for friendships.

Pause and Reflect

Write out a description of a person you know who walks with poise and yet keeps their sense of humor. Then, consider: Have they had an easy life? How have their difficulties strengthened their faith?

Pray

Lord Jesus, I praise You for Your promise that You will strengthen me and help me. You will uphold me with Your righteous right hand. I know that it is Your Spirit that strengthens me and helps me to walk with dignity. I pray, Lord, that You would show me actions that would take away from the dignity You have designed for me. Things like speaking without thinking, cynicism, or sarcasm. Instead, fill me with Your Spirit so that I might bless others with my humor, my words, and my actions. Above all else, I pray that I would trust You more and lean into You continually, no matter what is happening in my life.

"A good friend is someone who loves and fears God, which gives her a redeemed perspective of her friends."

Susie Larson

Bestselling Author, Radio Host

Closing Thoughts

Friends, thanks for joining me through these thirty days of practices for deeper friendships. I pray that you've enjoyed the stories: gum in the hair, belly dancers, friends who plan to meet for lunch but then show up at different places, and all the other stories included. But beyond the fun stories, I hope you have gleaned principles to guide you in being a good friend to others—principles like listening, empathizing, not over-functioning, setting and respecting boundaries, and slowing down and being available.

I pray that you see that God has given us the gift of friendships to inspire and encourage us. He brings friends in all different seasons and at all different times to enrich our lives and enhance our growth.

As I look back on years of friendship, I am eternally grateful to those I call friends. Each one has been a treasure. Some friendships have been brief; others have lasted for years, but all are precious to me. I realize that at times my friendships have appeared random—I was not even looking for a new friendship but one developed. Looking back, I believe God Himself orchestrated those relationships so that my life would produce a beautiful worship chorus. Each friend has played a different part.

C. S. Lewis wrote this about the formation of friendships:

> We think we have chosen our peers. In reality, a few years' difference in the dates of our births, a few more miles between certain houses,

> the choice of one university instead of another . . . the accident of a topic being raised or not raised at a first meeting . . . any of these chances may have kept us apart. But, for a Christian, there are, strictly speaking, no chances. A secret Master of Ceremonies has been at work. Christ, who said to the disciples, "Ye have not chosen me, but I have chosen you," can truly say to every group of Christian friends "Ye have not chosen one another but I have chosen you for one another." The Friendship is not a reward for our discriminating and good taste in finding one another out. It is the instrument which God reveals to each of us the beauties of others.[1]

In your life, the same holds true. Each friend brings different strengths, weaknesses, and perspectives. But each one can be used by God to help transform you into the image of His Son, Jesus Christ.

I pray as we conclude our journey together that you will be intentional to become friend-wise. May this book serve as a resource you return to again and again to help you hone the skills of developing deep friendship. I pray you slow down enough to treasure each friend God brings into your life and that each one will draw you closer to the dearest friend of all, Jesus Christ.

Grace and joy to you,
Becky

Acknowledgments

Writing *Friend-Wise* has been a joy! Since book writing never happens alone, it's been wonderful to lean into community! I am so thankful for:

My husband, Steve. Babe, thank you for patiently cheering me on with each new writing project. I'm so thankful for our journey together! I love you so much!

My kids,

Bethany and Chris. I am so thankful for the way you two live out the gospel, serving families in the foster care system. You are amazing parents to your five boys and wonderful friends to so many. Love and appreciate you both so much!

JJ and Shaina. I am so grateful for your commitment to Jesus, to Compel Global, and to prayer. You both have such strong gifts of leadership and wisdom. I love your compassionate hearts and your diligence in parenting your boys. I love you both so much!

Stefanie and Dave. It's been so fun over the past year and a half to watch how both your careers have expanded and your leadership roles have grown. I love how you both have such a heart for your community. You are great parents to your four kids. I love you both so much!

Keri and Zach. I'm so grateful for your heart for worship and integrity in the nonprofit realm. God has taken you on quite the journey this past year and it has been a joy to watch you lean into Him and trust Him. I love how intentional you are with your kids. I love you both so much!

To my amazing grandkids, who keep me young and laughing. I'm so thankful for each one of you and all I get to see God do in your lives: Charlie, Ty, Josh, Selah, Zach, Theo, Noah, Rayna, Cayden, Kinley, Tori, Melody, Asher, and Austin. Whew! You guys delight my heart! I pray for each of you every day and trust that you will continue to walk with Jesus and serve Him. I love you beyond what you can imagine!

To my amazing agent and trusted friend, Blythe Daniel! Blythe, I am so grateful for your passion for my books but also for your heart of prayer. So many times we have had the privilege of going before God together. You are a treasure, and I love you!

To all the amazing men and women at Moody Publishers, Judy Dunagan, my dear friend who first acquired this book. Erin Davis who became my acquisitions editor and quickly became my friend. Amanda Cleary Eastep for her attention to detail in editing, and to Hope Lemerand, who has helped me countless times think through all the marketing issues. I am so grateful for each of you in the journey!

To all my precious friends who have helped me become a better friend: Judy, Jill, Keri, Gayle, Linda, and many others. I am incredibly grateful for each of you!

NOTES

Introduction

1. Eric Barker, "Happy Thoughts: Here Are the Things Proven to Make You Happier," *Time*, April 4, 2014, http://time.com/49947/happy-thoughts-here-are-the-things-proven-to-make-you-happier/.
2. William F. Arndt et al., *A Greek-English Lexicon of the New Testament and Other Early Christian Literature* (University of Chicago Press, 2000), 219. *Hokmah* (wise) refers to godly cleverness and skill, which results in practical action. The one who hears (Prov. 8:33; 23:19; 27:11) will be industrious, will know how to talk, and his will, will be in captivity to God's. R. Laird Harris, Gleason L. Archer Jr., and Bruce K. Waltke, eds., *Theological Wordbook of the Old Testament* (Moody, 1999), 283.

Chapter 4

1. Adrian Rogers, "How to Guard Your Heart," February 17, 2023, https://www.biblestudytools.com/bible-study/topical-studies/how-to-guard-your-heart.html.
2. Peter Scazzero, *Emotionally Healthy Relationships Day by Day* (Zondervan, 2017), 50.

Chapter 5

1. Becky Harling, *Cultivating Deeper Connections in a Lonely World* (Moody, 2024), 77.

Chapter 9

1. Geri Scazzero, *The Emotionally Healthy Woman* (Zondervan, 2010), 146.

Chapter 14

1. Scazzero, *Emotionally Healthy Relationships*, 87.

Chapter 17

1. "Stress Relief from Laughter? It's No Joke," Mayo Clinic, September 22, 2023, https://www.mayoclinic.org/healthy-lifestyle/stress-management/in-depth/stress-relief/art-20044456.

Chapter 19

1. Becky Harling, *How to Listen So People Will Talk* (Bethany House, 2017), 91.
2. Scazzero, *Emotionally Healthy Relationships*, 132.

Chapter 20

1. https://www.encyclopedia.com/humanities/dictionaries-thesauruses-pictures-and-press-releases/gossip-0

Chapter 21

1. I also told this story in my book *Cultivation Deeper Connections in a Lonely World* (Moody, 2024), 132.
2. Donald Moynihan, "Virtue Rewarded: Helping Others at Work Makes People Happier," University of Wisconsin-Madison, July 29, 2013, https://news.wisc.edu/virtue-rewarded-helping-others-at-work-makes-people-happier/.
3. Asheritah Ciuciu, *Delighting in Jesus* (Moody, 2024), 246.

Chapter 25

1. Daniel Babaris, "The Man Who Found Forrest Fenn's Treasure," *Outside*, December 9, 2020, https://www.outsideonline.com/outdoor-adventure/exploration-survival/forrest-fenn-treasure-jack-stuef/.

Chapter 26

1. Harling, *Cultivating Deeper Connections*, 110.
2. Alli Worthington, DATE?, https://www.instagram.com/alliworthington.

Chapter 29

1. Rick Hellman, "How to Make Friends? Study Reveals How Many Hours It Takes," KU News, March 28, 2018, https://news.ku.edu/news/article/2018/03/06/study-reveals-number-hours-it-takes-make-friend.

Chapter 30

1. Becky Harling, "3 Prayers of Blessing to Strengthen Your Friendships," (blog), July 29, 2024, https://beckyharling.com/3-prayers-of-blessing-to-strengthen-your-friendships/.

Closing Thoughts

1. C. S. Lewis, *The Four Loves* (HarperOne, 2017), 10.